Better Homes and Gardens.

Best of
CHRISTMAS
IDEAS

contents

4 Holiday Homes

6 Easy Elegance
You'll love our simple handcrafted ideas that emphasize the timeless holiday hues of deep red and crisp white.

16 Merry & Bright
Give traditional decor a fresh and fun new look with the addition of bright florals.

28 Swedish Noel
A nod to Nordic ways creates a cheerful stage for holiday entertaining. You'll find a smorgasbord of ideas for keeping everyone's spirits extra bright.

40 Tradition with a Twist
Add lime green to the classic holiday colors of red and forest green for a look that's fresh and fun but still satisfies your tradition-bound family.

52 A Warm & Cozy Christmas
Warm the heart and soul with a casual soup supper that takes the chill off. Our recipes and decorating tips make it easy to gather the family for a day of good food and good fun.

64 Tradition with a Twist of Lime
Decorator Shana Smith adorns her home in a unique palette of black, white, and lime green.

11
20

88
102

70 Deck the Halls

72 Fresh, Fast & Fabulous
Enliven holiday decorating by bringing fresh flowers, berries, and greenery to your table.

80 Well-Rounded Wreaths
With this trio of wreaths, you're bound to find a design to suit your Christmas scheme, whether it's modern, traditional, or simply elegant.

84 Poinsettia Pointers
Learn how to pick the perfect poinsettia (and keep it that way). Then discover wonderful ways to use this showy bloom as a festive seasonal accent.

88 Holiday Harvest
Nature provides seasonal elements for trees and wreaths that can augment a warm and cozy theme.

96 Outdoor Decor
These easy greenery and lighting ideas make your home as warm and inviting on the outside as it is inside.

100 Christmas Treats

102 Sweet Tidings
Downright delectable, these sugary snacks and desserts are sure to delight.

108 Simple Sweets
Dazzle and delight your family and guests with these sinfully sweet (and deceptively simple) chocolate treats.

116 Gourmet Gifts
Presentation matters: These goodies are as tasteful as they are tastefully given.

130 Festive Tables

132 Serving Up Style
A holiday feast should also be a feast for the eyes. Get great, fast, and fresh ideas for setting a holiday table to remember.

142 Blue Christmas
Prepare the guest list; then use our monogrammed projects in shades of blue and green to make your party a success.

150 3 Seasonal Settings
Take your pick from country, classic, and retro for handmade dressings on your Christmas table.

160 Quick-as-a-Wink

162 Jingle Bells
A favorite of all ages, jingle bells add a fun musical note to your decor.

170 Graceful Garlands
Tinsel and beaded garlands aren't just for trees. Use them to wrap your whole home with holiday touches.

176 Blue Ice
Build your holiday color scheme on the crystal-clear blues found in ice and snow. Just imagine snowflake trims on packages, wreaths made of clear blue and white balls, and stockings edged with icy beads.

184 Wrapping Up the Season
Show your family and friends how special they are when you present them with a package worth remembering.

190 Sources

holiday homes

Usher in the Christmas season with merry decorations for every room of your home.

easy elegance

Seek inspiration from timeless design elements and the simplest hand-crafting supplies to fashion holiday decor that's rich in beauty but easy on the budget.

STYLED BY: **CATHY KRAMER**   PHOTOGRAPHED BY: **KIM CORNELISON**   WRITTEN BY: **KRISTIN SCHMITT**

luxurious wrap

Reach into your decorating leftovers for an elegant wrapping alternative. Rich in pattern and texture, wallpaper forms a handsome outer shell that works nicely with silk-ribbon bows, pretty paper doilies (layered with spray adhesive), or scrapbooking sticker labels, *opposite*.

traditional trim

Breathe new life into the classic Christmas palette by posing handmade ornaments solely of deep reds and crisp whites against an evergreen canvas. Then coordinate with beautiful packages in the same colors.

Achieve an elegant look with ease by keeping a consistent palette and introducing interest through texture.

fashion statement Accessorize your tree as you would your best holiday attire by including some jeweled accents. This dainty wreath, *above*, is simply a pattern of petite pearlized beads threaded on a wire bracelet form and topped with a delicate ribbon bow.

pretty package Double the sentiment of gift-giving by presenting the treasure inside a hand-decorated package. Paint a papier-mâché box from the crafts store with red and white acrylic paints, *above right*. Run a strip of white felt through a die-cut machine to punch out snowflake or other holiday motifs, and glue the band around the box.

seasonal bouquet Fashion this holiday version of a cheerful May Day basket, *right*, by tucking a petite silk nosegay into a cone formed from embossed felt.

easy accents A piece of toile pattern trimmed from a dinner napkin and decoupaged onto a basic ball becomes an elegant ornament with ease, *opposite*. A spray-painted cap adds a customized touch. To fashion the retro ribbon-candy styled ornament, see the instructions on page 12.

Classic motifs are favorites this season. Include lace, toile, and pearls in creative new ways for fresh beauty.

simple embellishment A polished package can be the product of the simplest supplies picked up at crafts and scrapbooking stores. These wallpaper-wrapped gift boxes, *opposite,* earn their elegant touches from raw silk ribbon and a crystal embellishment (top), a lace-inspired sticker (middle), and a poinsettia formed from square paper frames (bottom).

paper masterpieces Don't dismiss paper-crafted ornaments as childish or simplistic. Today's impressive array of scrapbooking papers can create high-end looks. See the instructions on page 12 for these designs, *above.*

less is more Sometimes the most formal look can be achieved by simply tying up a package wrapped in tone-on-tone wallpaper with a decorative fabric ribbon, *above right.*

one-of-a-kind Visitors will marvel at your tree trimmings as if you shopped the most exquisite boutiques. Surprise them when you tell them that you handcrafted these charming ornaments, *right,* following the instructions on page 12.

1. Painted Ornament

Provided by Plaid Enterprises

MATERIALS

- Red and white round glass ornaments
- Red and white spray paint
- Ultra-fine-point permanent marking pen
- Cotton swabs
- Rubbing alcohol
- Plaid Tip Pen set
- Dowel stick or pencil
- Coffee cup or paper cup
- Small items, such as marbles, to weight the cup
- Folk Art Enamels Paint: #4001 Wicker White and #4006 Engine Red

INSTRUCTIONS

Note: Ornaments with an outer glaze or frost matte finish are not suitable for this technique. To determine the finish on your ornament, remove the metal top and brush the exposed top of the ornament with a cotton swab dipped in alcohol. If the finish is not altered, the ornament has an acceptable finish.

Spray-paint the metal top white for red ornaments and red for the white ones.

Using the marking pen, mark four equally spaced dots around the neck of the ornament. Making light marks with the marking pen, follow each dot down the sides of the ornament, stopping three-quarters of the way. Use a cotton swab dipped in alcohol to erase and redraw the lines if necessary.

Referring to the photographs, randomly draw swirls, circles, lines, dots, and squiggles with the marking pen within the quadrants.

Follow the manufacturer's instructions with the Tip Pen set to prepare the paint bottles. Use the second largest micro tip from the set.

Prepare a drying area for your ornament by placing a dowel stick in a weighted cup.

Hold the ornament in your hand, supporting it with your thumb and fingertips, and begin painting the design. Do not touch the micro tip to the ornament; let the paint flow onto the drawn lines. Turn the ornament as you paint your way around the design. Paint the top section of the ornament first; allow it to dry on the dowel for 2 to 3 hours. Paint the bottom section in the same way. When dry, replace the metal top.

2. Evergreen Tree

Designed by Mary Heaton

MATERIALS

- Green patterned paper
- White card stock
- Snowflake and tree die-cut shapes (available at scrapbooking stores)
- Straight edge and crafts knife
- Small hole punch
- Glue gun and hotmelt adhesive
- Thin monofilament string
- Embroidery needle
- Small green bead
- Medium-width ribbon

INSTRUCTIONS

Note: If your patterned paper is one-sided, use spray adhesive and join the wrong sides together on two sheets of paper.

Die-cut two trees from green paper and one snowflake from white paper.

Using the punch, make a hole in the center of the snowflake.

With scissors, cut a 1½-inch slit down the center of one tree, starting at the tip of the tree. Make a 1⅛-inch slit on the center of the other tree, starting at the trunk. Slip the two trees together to form a dimensional tree.

Insert the tree trunk through the hole in the snowflake, and glue the trunk sections to the bottom of the snowflake.

Thread a needle with monofilament line. Push the needle through the tip of one tree; add the bead, and then sew the monofilament to the center of the ribbon and secure. Tie the ribbon in a knot to form a hanging loop.

3. Snowflake Tree

Designed by Jennifer Keltner

MATERIALS

- Two 4-inch and four 2¾-inch die-cut snowflake shapes
- Embroidery needle
- Long-eye beading needle
- White embroidery floss
- Ten 10-mm-round white pearls
- Medium-width ribbon

INSTRUCTIONS

To give shape to the tree, slightly trim the tips from one large and one small snowflake shape. Use the embroidery needle to push a small hole through the center of each snowflake.

Thread the beading needle with an 18-inch length of embroidery floss. Slip a pearl onto the floss. Carefully remove the needle, and then rethread it with both ends of the floss. The ends of the floss should be even.

Thread the needle through the bottom of a large snowflake; add two pearls. Thread the needle through the remaining snowflakes, from largest to smallest, adding two pearls between each shape. Finish with a pearl at the top. Sew through the center of the ribbon and secure the thread.

4. Candy Twist

Designed by Brenda Lesch

MATERIALS

- Spray adhesive
- Wide, medium, and narrow ribbon
- Water-soluble marking pen
- Long-eye beading needle
- White embroidery floss
- Eleven 10-mm-round pearls

INSTRUCTIONS

Glue the medium-width ribbon to the center of the wide ribbon. Trim the length to measure 16½ inches.

Using the pen and a ruler, mark dots down the center of the ribbon at 1½-inch intervals on both sides of the ribbon. Thread the beading needle with an 18-inch length of embroidery floss. Slip a pearl onto the floss. Carefully remove the needle, and then rethread it with both ends of the floss. The ends of the floss should be even.

Push the needle from one side of the ribbon through the other side at the first mark (the first pearl is now at the bottom of the ornament); add a pearl. Push the needle from the one side of the ribbon through to the other side at the second mark; add a pearl.

Continue until you have 11 pearls on the string.

To finish, secure the thread and attach a hanging ribbon.

5. Paper Poinsettia

Designed by Laura Collins

MATERIALS

- Two sheets of red card stock
- Straightedge and crafts knife
- Double-stick tape
- Glue gun and hotmelt adhesive
- Rhinestone brad

INSTRUCTIONS

Cut two 6-inch squares from the red paper.

Referring to the diagram, *page 15,* use a light pencil to divide one square into quadrants (this is the A side). Turn the square over; this time divide it diagonally into quadrants (this is the B side). Draw a 1½-inch-wide border around the inside of the square, creating a smaller 3-inch square in the center. Cut out the 3-inch center, making a frame. Erase one of the lines on the A side of the frame. Repeat for the other 6-inch square. Using the straight edge and a crafts knife, lightly score along the penciled lines. Fold the lines along the scored edges. Note: Each frame will be folded to create one half (four petals) of the poinsettia.

Cut three ½-inch pieces of tape. Place the frame on a flat surface with the A side down and the unscored side closest to you. Place the tape next to the folds as shown on the diagram (you can place the tape on either side of the scored lines). Fold the paper along one scored line with the tape in between; repeat for the other two scored lines. As you work, let the petals fold over to the A side. Turn

the shape to the A side. Using hot glue, secure the three inner points of the petals to the center of the unscored edge. One half of the poinsettia is completed.

Repeat the instructions for the other half. Glue the halves together, and then use a rhinestone brad for the center.

6. Tassel Trim

Designed by Artful Offerings

MATERIALS

- One 4½×18-inch strip each of red and dark red wool felt (or ivory and dark ivory)
- Hanging and trim ribbons
- Glue gun and hotmelt adhesive
- Wooden bead

INSTRUCTIONS

Mark an 18-inch long line 1⅛ inch from the top long edge of each felt strip. Make ½-inch cuts, starting at the bottom edge and stopping at the marked line. Stack the two felt strips, matching all the edges.

Fold the hanging ribbon in half; glue the cut ends in one corner of the felt, ½ inch down from the top edge.

Begin gluing and tightly rolling the tassel top, stopping ½ inch from the end. Wrap the top with trim, tucking and gluing the ends in place. Slip a bead over the top of the ribbon hanging loop.

7

8

9

7. Christmas Cardinal & Dove

Designed by Artful Offerings

MATERIALS

- Red or ivory wool felt
- Stiff interfacing
- Dark burgundy print fabric (for the cardinal only)
- Red or ivory embossed paper
- Double-stick fusible web
- Matching sewing thread
- Small beads for eyes
- Narrow hanging ribbon
- Glue gun and hotmelt adhesive

INSTRUCTIONS

Use the pattern on *page 15* to cut out two birds from the wool felt. Cut one bird ¼-inch smaller from the interfacing, and cut two wings from the embossed paper. For the cardinal, cut two face triangles from the print fabric.

Following the manufacturer's directions, apply fusible web to the wrong side of the felt birds, reversing the direction of one. For the cardinal, apply fusible web to the face triangles and fuse to the bird shape.

Using thread and needle, attach the bead eyes. Fold the hanging ribbon in half and place ½ inch from the top center of the bird. Lay the interfacing shape on top, and then lay the second felt bird shape on top. Carefully fuse the shapes together. Glue the wings to each side of the bird.

---

8. Toile Ornament

Provided by Plaid Enterprises

MATERIALS

- Round ornaments
- Red and white spray paint
- Medium-size drinking cups with 3-inch-diameter openings
- Toile napkins
- Flat artist's brush
- Decoupage medium

INSTRUCTIONS

Remove the ornament tops and spray-paint some with red, others with white.

To steady the ornaments, place them top side down into the cups.

Cut out images from the napkins and lay them right side down into the palm of your hand. Brush a thin coat of decoupage medium on the image, and carefully press it onto the ornament, smoothing wrinkles.

Allow ornaments to thoroughly dry in the cups. Replace the painted ornament tops.

9. Nosegay

Designed by Tari Colby

MATERIALS

- 9×12-inch pieces of fusible web, red vellum paper, and red embossed felt
- 8-mm textured red pearl
- Matching sewing thread
- Glue gun and hotmelt adhesive
- Narrow ribbon
- Polyester fiberfill (optional)
- Silk flowers

INSTRUCTIONS

Following the manufacturer's instructions, fuse the vellum to the wrong side of the felt. Photocopy the full-size pattern on *page 15*. Use the pattern to cut out one shape from the felt. Place the shape, vellum side up, on a flat surface. Thread the pearl on a length of thread; glue the ends to the vellum side of the shape with the pearl just below the point. Roll and glue the shape into a thin cone.

Glue hanging ribbon loops to the sides of the cone. Stuff cone with fiberfill. Run glue around the top inside edge of the cone and insert the bouquet.

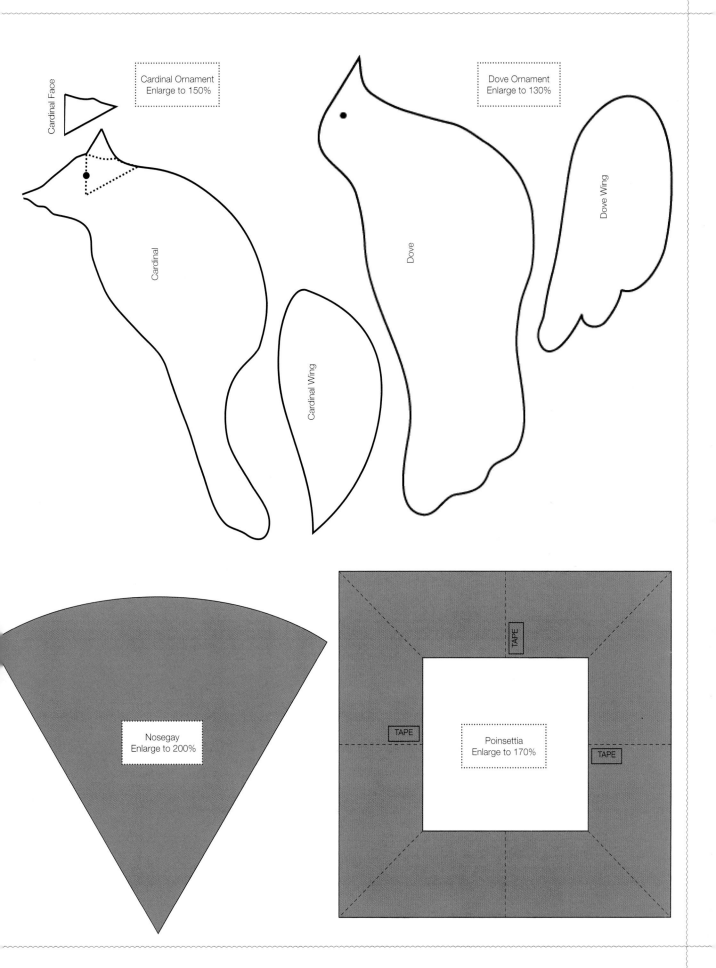

Cardinal Face

Cardinal Ornament
Enlarge to 150%

Cardinal

Cardinal Wing

Dove Ornament
Enlarge to 130%

Dove

Dove Wing

Nosegay
Enlarge to 200%

TAPE

TAPE

Poinsettia
Enlarge to 170%

TAPE

Merry & Bright

Hot hues of red and green provide a welcome update for one *family's traditional* and true holiday decor.

VENTLING   PHOTOGRAPHED BY **KIM CORNELISON**   WRITTEN BY **JODY GARLOCK**

The Romp family's living room staircase is always adorned with an evergreen swag at Christmastime. This year, a layer of bells of Ireland accentuated by big red bows lends a surprising boost of color and texture.

INSTRUCTIONS BEGIN ON PAGE 26.

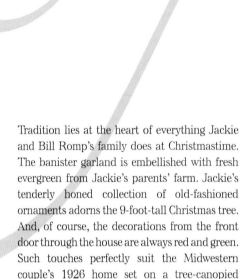

Tradition lies at the heart of everything Jackie and Bill Romp's family does at Christmastime. The banister garland is embellished with fresh evergreen from Jackie's parents' farm. Jackie's tenderly honed collection of old-fashioned ornaments adorns the 9-foot-tall Christmas tree. And, of course, the decorations from the front door through the house are always red and green. Such touches perfectly suit the Midwestern couple's 1926 home set on a tree-canopied street. "Christmas has always been very special to our family," Jackie says.

Though Jackie wears the label of chief merrymaker, creating a home brimming with Christmas spirit is a family affair. Shortly after the Thanksgiving leftovers disappear, Jackie and Bill drag boxes from the basement to the floor near the tree in the living room and unwrap hundreds of Jackie's ornaments. After eyeing their favorites, the couple's children—Jack and Jane—have the honor of hanging them. "We make it a family thing for as long as

the kids last, which is usually about an hour," Jackie says.

It's the children who inspire Jackie to make such an effort to incorporate traditions that many people push aside in the hustle-bustle of the holidays. And it's because of her children that Jackie welcomed the chance to try something new when decking the halls. With the help of designer Wanda Ventling, Jackie's holiday decor took a playful turn with a crisp, clean design and a palette that features brighter reds and limey greens. "This is a traditional home and in general, I'm traditional, but I like the clean lines and the new colors—it's something that gives traditional a twist or makes it fresh and young," Jackie says. "Especially with kids in the house, it's fun to make it bright and cheerful."

Ventling didn't look far for inspiration. The lime greens and reds in the fabrics and accents in the home's everyday decor helped the holiday decorations transition to an upbeat tempo without becoming so modern that they

Beaded topiaries lend a dose of holiday spirit to a table in the sunroom. The trees were made by wrapping different-size plastic-foam cones with beaded garland and then painting them to achieve a luster. Wrapped packages in various sizes complete the vignette.

French doors leading to the sunroom are pretty as a package with ribbon looped around each door. The ribbon is tied into a bow at the upper one-third of each door and adorned with gift tags declaring "Merry Christmas" to all. **Opposite:** A simple bells of Ireland swag replaces the usual evergreen on the mantel to lighten the mood. White pottery from Jackie's collection holds festive red and green ornaments. Vibrant red carnation wreaths add the finishing touch.

Symbolizing *good luck and fortune,* bells of Ireland provide a fun punch of color.

were out of sync with the classic setting. Ventling set the pace with bells of Ireland, known for their showy spikes symbolizing good luck. "It's probably my favorite color," Jackie says of the flower's limey hue. Layered with pine branches that wrap the staircase and form swags elsewhere in the home, the bells of Ireland provide an unexpected pop of color and texture and fill the air with their spicy scent. Though evergreens make an occasional appearance, traditional red poinsettias are absent. Instead, Ventling introduced bright red carnations for wreaths and topiaries.

In the sunroom, tasteful topiaries shift to the beaded variety with tree-shape tabletop gems that remind Jackie of the beaded ornaments her grandmother gave her as a child. These beaded beauties are less labor-intensive than the handmade ornaments Jackie's grandmother crafted. Ventling wrapped beaded garland around plastic-foam cones and painted the beads to add luster. The packages wrapped in spunky shades of red and green placed next to the miniature trees are a lively addition to the grouping and also are scattered throughout other rooms as inexpensive decorations.

Vintage pottery
decorated for the
Christmas season
visually connects
the dining table and
fireplace mantel.

Red carnation topiaries and swags of bells of Ireland tied with lime-green bows help break up the expanse of black furnishings in the dining room. Red-beaded garland placed atop the chandelier mimics holiday cranberries. **Opposite:** Subdued swirls in the table runner fabric lend a playful yet traditional detail to the dining table.

The home's front entrance announces the holiday scheme, while urns speak to its traditional architecture. The tree ornaments, carnation wreath, and topiaries are repeated indoors. **Opposite:** In the entry, a mirror placed atop a side table reflects the glow of candles in a grouping of hurricane glassware. Three of Jackie's glass ornaments dangle from the swag above the mirror, which is plumped up with bells of Ireland. Part of the mint family, the whimsical flower originated in western Asia—though its name implies otherwise.

Ornaments become the *finishing touches* on floral arrangements and even package trims.

But new touches don't trump old everywhere. Some of Jackie's treasured ornaments are the finishing details on swags and decorative packages. Ventling made sure the ornament-laden tree itself was still the star, although it, too, works with the revamped holiday decor.

Indeed, the playful look is classic enough to embrace the many traditions the Romps share. Every morning during December, Jackie and Bill hear footsteps rushing downstairs to the Advent box, where a piece of candy and a glass ornament await each of the children. "They're just as excited about what ornament they're going to get as they are the candy," Jackie says.

"It's a fun tradition." One evening during the month, Jackie gets out the tub of wrapping paper and allows the kids to help wrap gifts for their grandparents and others—a lesson designed to inspire an appreciation for giving. And on Christmas Eve, the family strolls through the neighborhood, which is always aglow in luminaries.

For Jackie, honoring old traditions while welcoming new ones is what makes the season so special. "I hope that someday my children will have fond memories of growing up with these traditions and remember the magic of Christmas," she says.

Carnation Wreath

Shown on *page 21.*

MATERIALS

- 12- and 16-inch-diameter florist's-foam wreaths
- 8-inch-diameter florist's-foam balls
- Carnations
- Small pruning shears

INSTRUCTIONS

Soak the florist's-foam shape in water following the manufacturer's instructions. Trim the carnations to about 3 inches. The 12-inch-diameter wreaths displayed on the mantel and the round orbs on the table require about 50 carnations each. The 16-inch-diameter wreath shown on the front door uses approximately 80 carnations. Insert the carnations into the form until the surface is covered. To prolong the freshness of the carnations, store the arrangements in a cool area when not in use. Artificial flowers may be used as well.

Beaded Trees

Shown on *page 19.*

MATERIALS

- 12-, 16-, and 20-inch plastic-foam cones
- Plastic-bead garlands in two different diameters
- Crafts glue
- Moss-color acrylic paint
- Pearl aerosol paint
- Glaze
- Foam brush
- Micro fine silver glitter

INSTRUCTIONS

Wrap and glue the plastic-bead garlands around the cone, alternating the size used to create a stripe effect until the entire cone is covered. Let the adhesive dry. Line a shallow box with newspaper and place the cone in the box. Spray a base coat of pearl paint, which will make covering the bead surface with acrylic paint easier. Mix two parts acrylic paint with one part water. Paint the cone, taking care to press the brush between the beads to apply some paint to the plastic-foam base. Let dry. If needed, apply another coat of the paint mixture for solid coverage. Once the paint has dried, apply the glaze to the tree with a brush. Immediately sprinkle a heavy coat of glitter onto the wet glaze. Let dry thoroughly.

1. Gift Tags

MATERIALS

- Computer
- Green card stock
- Crafts glue
- Micro fine silver glitter
- Hole punch
- Red ribbon

INSTRUCTIONS

On your computer, create a tag shape. Our door tag measures 5×8 inches and the package tags are 2×4 inches. Using Edwardian Script ITC font, add a message or a name to the center of the tag. Print the shapes on green card stock and cut out. Apply a border design with crafts glue and sprinkle with silver glitter. Let dry. Punch a hole at the top and thread a narrow ribbon through the tag to hang.

2. Bells of Ireland

MATERIALS

- Bells of Ireland stalks
- Crafts wire
- Ribbon
- Pine boughs approximately 18 inches long

INSTRUCTIONS

To make a swag garland, lay the bells of Ireland stalks on a flat working surface. Carefully wire the stalks end to end, overlapping the ends to keep the garland a uniform shape. If needed, a wire may be inserted in the stalks to provide stability. Hang as desired and embellish with ribbon bows.

For a one-direction swag as shown on the armoire on *page 23,* wire three or four bells of Ireland stalks and pieces of pine boughs together at one end. Form a wire hanging loop on the back side. Tie a ribbon bow and wire the bow to the swag.

For a two-directional swag as pictured above the mirror on *page 25,* wire the bells of Ireland and pine boughs following the directions above. Then repeat with the materials facing the opposite direction. Form a wire hanging loop on the back side. Assemble a ribbon bow and wire to the center of the swag.

Swedish Noel

Make your home merrier with a cheerful palette and natural trims inspired by *Swedish yuletide* traditions.

Striking in its simplicity, a Swedish-style Christmas boasts age-old elements that easily translate to suit modern-day celebrations. The customary candy-cane color scheme supplies a sprightly starting point for decking the halls, both here and abroad. In Sweden, bright-red apples, ribbons, and candles; scarlet tulips; Swedish flags; Dala horses; red-capped gnomes; ribbon-decked straw goats and straw hearts; snowflakes; and angels are likely to adorn everything from tabletops to tannenbaums.

We reinterpreted these Scandinavian trims and created decorations with a fresh, up-to-the-minute look and feel. You'll love how these red and white fabrics, fringes, papers, and ribbons spice up a conventional red and green Noel scheme. Take note of the natural wood finishes and rustic straw embellishments—although neutral in hue, they really pop when set against a backdrop of greenery.

Whether you'd like to add to your ornament collection or want to give a room an entirely new holiday view, we've got you covered. From cross-stitched stockings and a snowflake tablescape to straw wreaths and tree-motif pillows, you'll find a smorgasbord of ideas for keeping spirits and interiors extra bright during the upcoming season.

PRODUCED BY **LORI HELLANDER**   PHOTOGRAPHED BY **KIM CORNELISON**   WRITTEN BY **ANN WILSON**

Nordic Notions

Combine Swedish influences, a snowflake theme, and a dual-tone palette to set a celebratory stage for holiday entertaining. Dress a pine table with embroidered runners, snowflake-studded bowls, and wood-bead candlesticks. Suspend ribbon-joined straw wreaths in the windows and bedeck a fir tree with glittery red balls and straw, crafts-stick, and paper ornaments. Place the tree stand in a basket that echoes the wood tones elsewhere in the room.

Stitch Up Simplicity

Two crisp white linen runners are the perfect bases for a holiday tablescape, *above*. The beautiful—but easy enough for beginners—ribbon-embroidery snowflakes are striking embellishments.

Deck the Boughs

Our contemporary take on classic Swedish straw ornaments combines crafts sticks or clothespins with wood rounds to create different snowflake forms, *above right*. The star shapes provide neutral, clean-edge counterpoints to the busier baubles dressing the not-so-traditional tannenbaum.

Light Up the Night

Flickering red tapers are set in straw-hue candleholders constructed from unfinished wood dowels, beads, candle cups, and wheel bases, *right*. Tie the candlesticks to the tabletop theme by tacking on tiny snowflake cutouts.

Snowflake Settings

Fashion playful place settings by layering alternating red and white dishware atop large store-purchased paper snowflake mats. Give plain bowls a temporary wintry face-lift with the addition of snowflakes punched from red paper and glued in place. For a peppermint twist, add festive favors like these candy canes and evergreen sprigs bound together with string.

Deck the Halls

Arrange a welcoming vignette that offers a jolly välkommen to your guests, *this page.* Establish a cushy focal point by setting two plump color-reversed pillows on a white-painted bench. Cutout tree shapes pop thanks to red or white felt pieces behind the pillow front.

Festive Pair

Carry the fresh scheme to your mantel by pairing a quick-sew felt stocking with a mate in similar colors, *opposite.* Fill your sassy socks with Nordic trinkets—such as yule goats and straw ornaments—to step up the Swedish character.

INSTRUCTIONS BEGIN ON PAGE 34.

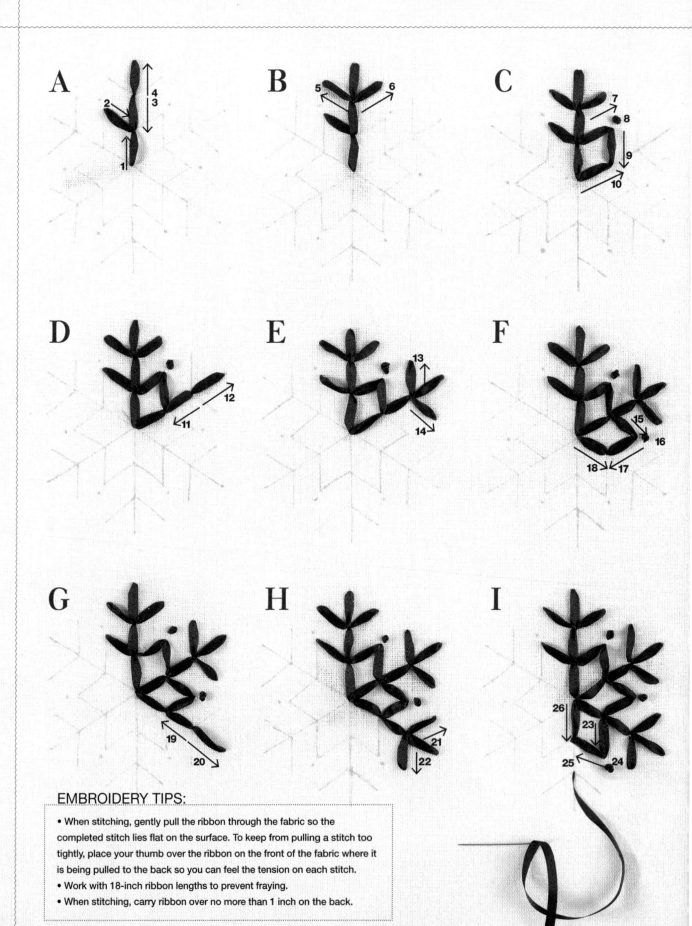

A

B

C

D

E

F

G

H

I

EMBROIDERY TIPS:

• When stitching, gently pull the ribbon through the fabric so the completed stitch lies flat on the surface. To keep from pulling a stitch too tightly, place your thumb over the ribbon on the front of the fabric where it is being pulled to the back so you can feel the tension on each stitch.

• Work with 18-inch ribbon lengths to prevent fraying.

• When stitching, carry ribbon over no more than 1 inch on the back.

Table Runner

Shown on *page 29.*

MATERIALS

- Purchased table runner
- 4-mm red embroidery ribbon
- Chenille or tapestry needle
- Water-soluble marker

INSTRUCTIONS

Because the fabric is light-colored, special attention should be paid to concealing the stitch transitions on the back of the fabric by weaving the ribbon back through previous stitches. For stitching progression, follow the step-by-step photo, *opposite,* which illustrates how the design is worked with the shortest possible transitions between stitches.

Enlarge the snowflake pattern on *page 39* using a photocopier. Tape the enlarged pattern to a window or place on a light box. Place the table runner over the pattern and trace the design onto the fabric using a water-soluble marker.

To stitch, bring the needle to the front of the fabric at 1 and make a straight stitch. Work a backstitch, bringing the needle up at 2 and taking it through the fabric at the end of the stitch 1. Continue working backstitches, bringing the needle up at 3 and taking it through the fabric at the intersection of stitches 1 and 2, and then bringing the needle up at 4 and back down through the fabric at the end of stitch 3.

Continue embroidering with backstitches, following the numbered sequence and the direction of the arrows, making French knots at dots on the pattern. This completes one half of the snowflake.

To finish the snowflake, turn the design around 180 degrees. The last stitch on the first half of the snowflake (stitch 26) now becomes stitch 1 on Diagram A and stitch 25 becomes stitch 2. Stitch the second half of the snowflake, following the numbered sequence on Diagrams A–I, beginning with stitch 3.

FRENCH KNOT:

Bring the needle to the front of the fabric and loosely wrap the ribbon one to two times around the needle, depending on the desired size of the knot. Hold the ribbon off to one side and push the needle through to the back directly next to the original entry point. Gently pull the needle through the wraps to form a complete knot.

Snowflake Dinnerware

Shown *below,* and on *page 31.*

MATERIALS

- Snowflake paper punch
- Red paper
- Crafts glue
- Sponge brush

INSTRUCTIONS

Punch snowflake shapes from red paper. Dilute crafts glue with water to the consistency of heavy cream. Working with one snowflake at a time, use the sponge brush to thoroughly coat the back side with glue. Place the snowflake on the bowl. Continue to apply snowflakes until the desired effect is achieved. Lightly brush glue over the top of each snowflake to seal. Let dry. Adhere leftover snowflakes on candlesticks, packages, or package tags. *Note:* The decorations on the dinnerware are not permanent and are not safe for dishwashing or for microwaving.

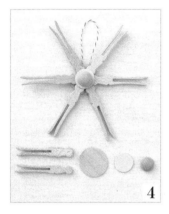

4

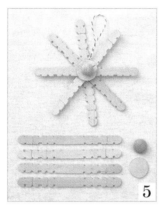

5

6

7

4. Clothespin Snowflake

MATERIALS

- Six small-size doll clothespins
- Glue gun and hotmelt adhesive
- Small- and medium-size wooden circles
- ½-inch-diameter button plug

INSTRUCTIONS

Glue the clothespins to the medium-size wooden circle, positioning them near the outside edge. Glue the small round shape to the center front of the snowflake, then glue the button plug in the center of the round.

5. Crafts-Stick Snowflake

MATERIALS

- Eight crafts sticks
- Glue gun and hotmelt adhesive
- Small- and medium-size wooden circles
- ½-inch-diameter button plug

INSTRUCTIONS

Overlap crafts sticks to form a snowflake shape, and glue it to the medium-size wooden circle. Glue the small-size wooden circle in the center of the snowflake and a button plug on top of that.

6. White Pillow

MATERIALS

- 1 yard of white felt
- Scraps of red felt
- Scalloped-edge scissors
- Matching sewing thread
- Fabrics glue
- 16-inch pillow form

INSTRUCTIONS

For the pillow front, cut a 17½×14-inch rectangle and a 17½×4-inch rectangle of white felt. Cut a 17½×¾-inch strip of red felt and use the scalloped-edge scissors to trim a decorative edge along one long side. Sandwich the strip of red felt between the white felt rectangles and sew together using a ¼-inch seam allowance. Enlarge the tree pattern on *page 39* using a photocopier; cut out the patterns. Trace the small tree pattern onto the back side of the pillow front and cut out the tree-

shape opening. Trace the large tree pattern onto red felt and cut out. Cut a 4½-inch long strip of white felt using the scalloped-edge scissors on each long edge. Glue the white felt strip on the back side of the tree-shape opening followed by the red felt tree shape.

For the pillow back, cut two 17½×9-inch rectangles of white felt. With right sides together, stitch the pillow back to the pillow front using a ¼-inch seam allowance, overlapping the pillow back pieces at the center back to create an opening for the pillow form. Turn right side out and insert pillow form. Note: For a more permanent pillow, substitute the fabrics glue with needle and thread.

7. Red Pillow

MATERIALS

- 1 yard of red felt
- Scraps of white felt
- Fabrics glue
- Red pom-pom trim
- Matching sewing thread
- 16-inch pillow form

INSTRUCTIONS

For the pillow front, cut a 17½-inch square of red felt. Enlarge the tree pattern on *page 39* using a photocopier; cut out the pattern. Trace the tree pattern twice onto the back side of the pillow front and cut out the tree-shape openings. Cut a 4½×10½-inch rectangle of white felt. Glue the white rectangle strip on the back side of the pillow front, covering the tree-shape openings. Cut a few pom-poms from the trim

8

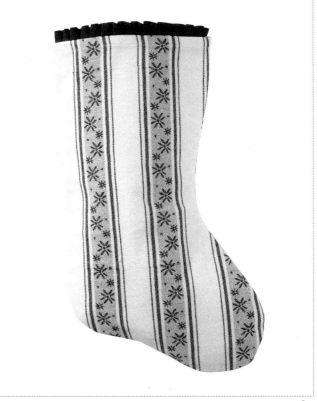

9

and glue them on the trees. Sew a 17½-inch length of pom-pom trim across the pillow front.

For the pillow back, cut two 17½×9-inch rectangles of red felt. With right sides together, stitch the pillow back to the pillow front using a ¼-inch seam allowance, overlapping the back pieces at the center back to create an opening for the pillow form. Turn right side out and insert pillow form. Note: For a more permanent pillow, substitute the fabrics glue with needle and thread.

----

8. Stitched Stocking
MATERIALS
- ½ yard white felt
- Red cotton embroidery floss
- Size 5 needle
- Matching sewing thread
- Scalloped-edge scissors
- Stiffened white crafts felt

INSTRUCTIONS
Cut five 17×2¼-inch strips of white felt. On each strip, fold back each raw long edge and press lightly. Measure and mark ½-inch spaces on each long side of the strips. Using red embroidery floss, stitch large X shapes to join the strips.

Enlarge the stocking pattern on *page 39* using a photocopier. Cut the stocking front out of the strip assembly and cut the stocking back out of white felt.

With right sides together and using a ¼-inch seam allowance, sew the stocking front to the back, leaving the top edges open. Trim the seams, and clip the curves. Turn the stocking right side out.

Fold the top edge of the stocking over ¼-inch and topstitch.

Using scalloped-edge scissors, cut a 3×19-inch length of stiffened white crafts felt for a stocking cuff. Stitch large X shapes along the center of the cuff strip. With right sides together and using a ¼-inch seam allowance, sew the short edges of the embroidered cuff strip together. Turn and press. Glue or hand-stitch the cuff to the top edge of the stocking.

----

9. Tea Towel Stocking
MATERIALS
- 2 tea towels
- Fusible web
- Matching sewing thread
- ½ yard red ruffled trim

INSTRUCTIONS
Iron fusible web to the back of each tea towel. Enlarge the stocking pattern on *page 39* using a photocopier. Cut the stocking front and back out of the web-backed tea towels.

With right sides together and using a ¼-inch seam allowance, sew the stocking front to the back, leaving the top edges open. Trim the seams, and clip the curves. Turn the stocking right side out; press. Fold the top edge of the stocking over ½-inch, pin the ruffled trim along the edge of the opening, and topstitch using a ⅜-inch seam allowance.

10. Tree Box

MATERIALS
- Scrapbooking pyramid box die cut
- White card stock
- Crafts knife
- Paper punch
- Double-stick tape
- Red and white narrow ribbon
- Square white box for tree base

INSTRUCTIONS

Punch a die-cut tree shape from paper. Enlarge the shape to the desired size using a photocopier. Trace the enlarged pattern onto white card stock and cut out using a crafts knife. Using a paper punch, make a hole in the top point of each box side. Fold the tabs and assemble the box using double-stick tape. To close the box, thread the ribbons through the prepunched holes and tie in a bow. Use double-stick tape to adhere the square box tree base to the bottom of the tree.

----

11. Candleholder

MATERIALS
- ½-inch-diameter dowel
- 2½-inch-diameter wheel
- Wood glue
- Seven wooden beads
- Small candle cup

INSTRUCTIONS

Glue the dowel into the hole in the center of the wheel; let dry. Place two narrow lines of wood glue along opposite sides of the length of dowel, and then thread the wooden beads onto the dowel. Wipe away any excess glue. Glue the candle cup onto the end of the dowel.

Paper Snowflakes

MATERIALS
- Red and white paper
- Scissors
- Small paper punch

INSTRUCTIONS

Measure and cut paper into a 9-inch square. Fold the square in half horizontally, then in half vertically. Rotate the folded square so that the center point is at the top, and then fold the square in thirds vertically. Cut out snowflake openings along the folded sides and trim the bottom edge as desired. Unfold the snowflake and punch a hole in one paper point for hanging. Note: If you do not want the folds to show, use the folded and cut snowflake for a template, trace it onto paper, and cut out using a crafts knife.

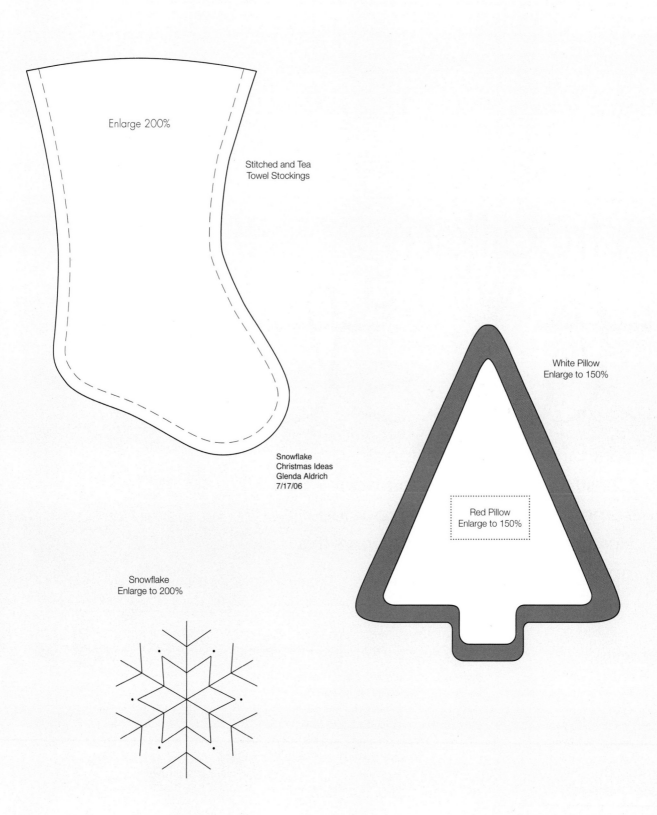

Enlarge 200%

Stitched and Tea
Towel Stockings

Snowflake
Christmas Ideas
Glenda Aldrich
7/17/06

White Pillow
Enlarge to 150%

Red Pillow
Enlarge to 150%

Snowflake
Enlarge to 200%

Written and produced by **WANDA J. VENTLING** Photography by **KIM CORNELISON**

tradition
with a
twist

Your family wants traditional
Christmas decorating. You want
something fresh and unexpected.
Here's how to have it both ways this
holiday season.

Lime green adds a designer
punch to the traditional
Christmas palette of red
and green. It's a fresh way
to update your traditional
holiday decorating without
starting over.

Lavish detail on holiday projects by using dressy trims and elegant fabrics.

Christmas red and green may be traditional, but they also can become boring. As interior design colors shift from year to year to stay fashionable, so can the shades of your holiday reds and greens. Instead of one green and one red, update your Christmas look with a fashion-forward color, such as the yellow-based green used here. Make sure your new color blends with traditional Christmas red and green.

Not sure of the hue you want? Look to color marketers, trendy retailers, and magazines to see what colors are hot this Christmas. When the new decorations arrive in stores this fall, make a scouting trip to find the freshest Christmas colors.

LEFT: Pinwheels of pleated ribbon look pretty on the tree and perfect on a gift box. Hot-glue the pleated ribbon to a cardboard circle, and cover the center with a smaller cardboard circle wrapped in ribbon and edged with trim. OPPOSITE: Quilted velvet looks beautiful as the basis for these elegant stockings. To finish the tops, sew triangles of satin in two colors; add tassel trim and ball fringe for a fancy finish.

Try these six strategies to incorporate the new hues into your classic Christmas decorating.

• **INTRODUCE THE NEW COLOR IN MEDIUM-SIZE DOSES:** ornaments, ribbons, fabrics, and fresh and artificial floral material. Add the new color using inexpensive ideas such as placing lime-green moss in containers and wrapping lime-green ribbons around packages. Don't throw out last year's decorations just because the color palette is altered a bit. Use new and old colors together. For example, create a cluster of balls by wiring new lime-color ornaments with Christmas-green balls.

• **INCORPORATE DECORATOR ELEMENTS INTO YOUR HOLIDAY SCHEME.** Animal prints, still hot in home decor, show up on these pages as printed black-and-white ribbons wrapped around boxed table favors. A touch of this pattern yields a big decorating return.

• **USE CLASSIC ORNAMENTS SUCH AS CHRISTMAS BALLS IN SHINY AND MATTE FINISHES.** Cluster the smallest balls with mixed greens; florist's wire holds up to a dozen balls tightly together. Traditional red glass balls, nearly the size of soccer balls, bring big doses of red to the tree on *page 40*; their grand scale makes them feel as fresh as the lime-color balls.

ABOVE LEFT: Create these ornaments in just a few minutes by hot-gluing velvet ribbon onto a cardboard base. The tiny covered button adds dressmaker detailing. LEFT: Create packages worth the wait to open using elegant ribbon formed into pleated bows and accented with covered buttons and sparkly fashion pins. OPPOSITE: For a designer look, wrap an inexpensive pillow with double-faced satin ribbon and add a purchased beaded tassel.

Buy pillows in holiday colors, and then decorate them to look like wrapped packages.

Start with plenty of greens to add luxury to the mantel. Two garland ropes were laid over one another below a large wreath. The red toile containers flanking the wreath were discount-store finds dressed up with ribbon and filled with paper whites.

Mixed flowers are easy to arrange for do-it-yourself designers. Look for a variety of shapes, and keep the palette simple, such as using white roses, stock, and ranunculus; red tulips; and lime-color greens.

• **MAKE THE NEW COLOR A PERMANENT PART OF YOUR HOLIDAYS** by crafting items from quality materials using time-honored techniques. For example, the stockings and ribbon ornaments in this story are made from luxurious fabrics and ribbon. The stocking design incorporates a jester's triangle, and the ornaments feature pleating and ruffling.

• **ADD A TOUCH OF DRAMA WITH A SURPRISE ELEMENT** such as an oversize black iron urn used as a tree base. Consider using garden urns, galvanized tubs, or any oversize container. Line each container with a plastic bucket or wastebasket to prevent water damage. Protect the floor underneath the container with heavy plastic trimmed close to the container's base. For an artificial tree, fit the trunk inside the container and secure it in place with sand and rocks. Test the tree to make sure it won't tip.

• **FRESHEN A TRADITIONAL LOOK WITH OVERSIZE CUSTOM-DESIGNED GREENERY AND FLORAL CREATIONS.** For example, two lengths of lush garland dress the fireplace mantel on *page 41,* creating a grand scale that matches the iron pieces on the mantel and in front of the firebox. Plan for a few large dramatic wreaths rather than lots of small pieces spread throughout the house.

OPPOSITE: Welcome dinner guests with sprigs of greens and berries tied to the backs of their chairs. Each mini bouquet takes only a few minutes to make.
ABOVE LEFT: Classic stripes decked with braids and tassels dress a simple white cloth. The green runners add a needed punch to the tabletop and pair nicely with the Christmas-red runner sewn in the same style.
LEFT: Send guests home with a remembrance of your good taste. These ribbon-wrapped boxes are made extraspecial with a wreath pencil drawing that was scanned and printed onto velum.

INSTRUCTIONS BEGIN ON PAGE 50.

TRADITION WITH A TWIST

RED & GREEN STOCKINGS
Shown *above,* and on *page 43.*

MATERIALS
For one stocking:
  Graph paper (optional)
  5⁄8 yard of red quilted fabric
  5⁄8 yard of red lining fabric
  1⁄8 yard of solid green fabric
  1⁄4 yard each of green and red
    check fabrics
  Scrap of dark green velvet
  Matching sewing thread
  1⁄2 yard of ball trim
  1⁄2 yard of 3-inch-wide feather trim
  Three 1 1⁄2-inch tassels

INSTRUCTIONS
Enlarge the stocking patterns on *page 51* using a photocopier; mark 1⁄2-inch seam allowances.

Cut a red stocking front and back and a red lining front and back. Cut two cuffs from solid green fabric for the cuff and cuff lining. Make a triangle pattern that measures 6 1⁄2 inches long and 4 inches at the wide end. Cut two triangles from the red check and four from the green check. Make a pattern for the heel, and cut one from the dark green velvet scrap.

Press under 1⁄2 inch on the inner edge of the heel. Position the heel wrong side down on the right side of the stocking front, aligning the outer edges; pin in place. Machine-sew the outer edge, and hand-sew the pressed edge.

Sew the stocking front to the back, leaving the top edge open. Trim the seams; clip the curves. Turn the stocking right side out.

Sew the stocking lining pieces together, leaving the top edge open. Trim the seam and clip the curves. Do not turn. Slip the lining inside the stocking with wrong sides facing, aligning the top edges. Baste the top edges together.

Cut a 1 1⁄2×6-inch strip of solid green fabric for the hanging loop. Press under 1⁄4 inch on each long edge of the strip. Fold the strip in half lengthwise, aligning the pressed edges; press again. Sew the pressed edges together opposite the fold. Fold the strip in half to form the loop. Aligning the raw edges, sew the loop to the top of the stocking.

Sew the same color points of the triangles together in pairs, leaving the top edges open. Trim the seams and corners. Turn the points right side out; press. Center the red point on the bottom long edge of the cuff lining with the raw edges even. Position the green points along the same edge of the cuff lining, overlapping the top side edges of the red point by 1 1⁄4 inches. Baste to the cuff lining. Stitch tassels to the triangle points.

Sew the cuff to the cuff lining at the bottom long edge, catching the points in the stitching. Turn the cuff right side out and press, directing the points away from the cuff. Baste the top edge of the cuff and lining together. Pin and sew the ball trim on the right side of the cuff. Position feather trim along the top edge; sew in place. Fold the cuff in half with right sides together; stitch short edges.

Slip the cuff inside the stocking with the right side of the cuff facing the stocking lining; sew the cuff to the stocking. Fold the cuff down over the right side of the stocking.

TAKE-HOME FAVOR BOXES
Shown on *page 49.*

MATERIALS
  1 1⁄2×3×3-inch cardboard boxes
  White acrylic paint
  Paintbrush
  Computer, scanner, and printer; or
    photocopy machine
  Copyright-free wreath sketch
  8 1⁄2×11-inch sheets of beige card
    stock
  Take-home treats
  1 1⁄2-inch-wide zebra-print ribbon
  5⁄8-inch-wide green message-print
    ribbon
  Tape
  Spray adhesive

INSTRUCTIONS
Paint the base of each box; let dry. Download a copyright-free wreath sketch: adjust to measure 2 inches in diameter. Position the image multiple times to fill an 8 1⁄2×11-inch sheet, leaving about 1 inch between the images. Print the images on beige card stock. Cut the card stock into 2 1⁄2-inch squares.

Fill each box with a take-home treat and wrap the 1 1⁄2-inch-wide ribbon around each box; tape. Wrap the 5⁄8-inch-wide ribbon around each box, centering it on the first ribbon; tape to secure. Use spray adhesive to adhere a wreath image to each box lid.

GREEN & RED TABLE RUNNER
Shown on *page 49.*

MATERIALS
  Two contrasting fabrics
  Matching sewing thread
  1 yard of 2 1⁄2-inch-wide tassel
    fringe for one runner
  1 yard of 2-inch-wide flat trim for
    one runner

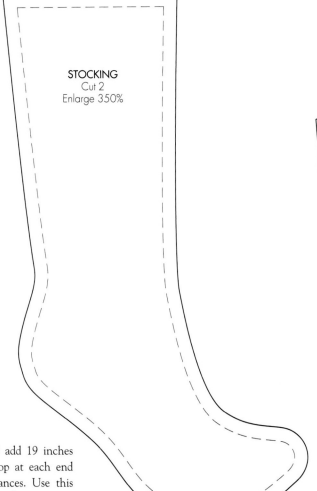

STOCKING CUFF
Cut 1
Enlarge 350%

STOCKING
Cut 2
Enlarge 350%

FARMHOUSE STOCKING
Cut 2

INSTRUCTIONS

Measure the table and add 19 inches to allow for a 9-inch drop at each end plus ½-inch seam allowances. Use this measurement to cut a 17½-inch-wide strip from each of the contrasting fabrics.

Pin and sew fringe on the right side of the fabric strip so the ends of the fringe are ½ inch or closer to each short edge. Pin and sew flat trim on the right side of the same fabric strip, leaving 1 inch between the fringe and the flat trim.

With right sides together, sew the two fabric strips together, taking care not to catch the tassels in the stitching and leaving a 4-inch opening on one side. Trim the seams and corners. Turn the table runner right side out; press. Slip-stitch the opening closed.

Christmas is a time for recalling special family memories and creating new ones. When family visits, the downtime spent at home is often the most special.

Written by **Amy Leibrock** Produced by **Lori Hellander** Photographed by **Greg Scheidemann**

a warm & cozy Christmas

Host effortless holiday get-togethers with make-ahead soups and meaningful decorations that celebrate family ties.

Handmade paper cones mixed with purchased red and white ball ornaments create a casual Christmas tree with a personal touch. A vintage tree topper adds to the charm. Keep the packages simple. Wrap them in kraft paper and add toppers for extra flair if you have time.

For many families, the weeks before Christmas include multiple—sometimes spur-of-the-moment—gatherings. Friends visit to deliver holiday greetings, family comes from out of town, and the neighbors stop by unannounced. To make sure every gathering is special, it helps to have good food on hand and a houseful of cozy decorations. Get the whole family involved along the way, and you'll make memories to last a lifetime.

To get started, designer Lori Hellander suggests decorating the Christmas tree with a bevy of balls to create a festive backdrop for a handful of special ornaments. One of her favorite homemade decorations

ABOVE LEFT: Spruce up a sofa or chair for the season with a wintry burlap pillow decorated with felt snowflakes. ABOVE RIGHT: To make a cone ornament, cover both sides of a 6-inch square of card stock with newspaper or scrapbooking paper. Hold the square by a point, twist into a cone shape, and secure with staples. Cut off excess to make a rounded top. Embellish with copies of photos, rickrack, and paper snowflakes. Glue or staple a yarn hanger inside the top of the cone. RIGHT: This soft garland gets its color from stacks of 1½-inch felt squares and purchased felt balls. Cut through multiple felt layers using a rotary cutter on a cutting board. String garland together with a needle and fishing line.

is a simple paper cone that can be covered with decorative paper and treasured family photos. Filled with candies or small pinecones, the cones can double as easy holiday favors for unexpected visitors. A soft, and surprisingly lightweight, felt garland wraps the tree in warmth.

As Christmas gets closer, children—and even adults—love the daily countdown of an Advent calendar. This year, try something new by using a bookshelf or a grouping of cubbyholes to hold small gifts, one for each December day until Christmas.

Take turns opening each day's present, or let a visitor do the honors. Be creative with what's inside each package—it can be something personal for the recipient or as simple as a candy cane.

OPPOSITE AND ABOVE LEFT: Christmas displays can be made in the most unlikely places. Designer Lori Hellander transformed this hutch into an Advent calendar. ABOVE LEFT: Make the "Noel" garland by printing letters onto card stock and stringing them from yarn. Finish off with a felt ball glued onto each end. ABOVE RIGHT AND RIGHT: Fill the nooks and crannies of the Advent calendar with a small token for each day.

ABOVE LEFT: Whether used as a centerpiece or atop a piano, miniature trees decorated with family photos are a way to remember loved ones and Christmases past. ABOVE RIGHT: Create unique stockings from a single fabric by changing the direction of the pattern. Label each with a photo of its owner to avoid mix-ups. LEFT: To make family-tree ornaments, slip photos into purchased photo holders or windowed note cards. Print text, such as names and dates, onto adhesive-backed paper; cut out, peel off backing, and press on ornament. Use scissors to clip each ornament's corners to make it look like a tag. Cut snowflake shapes from colored paper; glue to ornament.

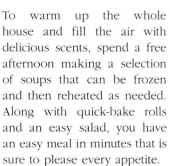

To warm up the whole house and fill the air with delicious scents, spend a free afternoon making a selection of soups that can be frozen and then reheated as needed. Along with quick-bake rolls and an easy salad, you have an easy meal in minutes that is sure to please every appetite.

Finish off a warm-and-cozy menu with an icy treat. Stock the freezer with a batch of ice cream sandwiches. Dress them up for the holidays by trimming them with crushed peppermint candy—a fun project for the kids. This make-ahead dessert will come in handy for impromptu gatherings and for satisfying a child's sweet tooth.

Share your meal on a table decorated with miniature trees with photo ornaments. Labeled with relatives' names, the trees

ABOVE LEFT: A make-ahead menu gives the family cook more time to socialize during a holiday gathering. ABOVE RIGHT: Combine shortcut products and homespun touches to make a special meal that everyone will love. Our Checkerboard Rolls use frozen roll dough and easy-to-assemble toppings. LEFT: In colder months, nothing warms the body and the soul like a hearty soup. Our Winter White Vegetable Soup (*left*) is reminiscent of snow, and Smoked Sausage-Split Pea Soup (*right*) conjures up the cozy warmth of a fire.

soup's on!

Avoid last-minute hassles, and enjoy every minute of your time with your family and friends by preparing much of our menu ahead of time.

✱ Make soups at your convenience and store them in the freezer for up to 3 months. Cook the soups for the minimum time given in the recipe. (Omit the beet in Winter White Vegetable Soup and the tortellini in Vegetable-Tortellini Soup.) Immediately place the soups in shallow containers and chill. Transfer chilled soups to freezer containers, cover, and freeze. To serve, thaw the soups in the refrigerator overnight. Reheat just before the party, bringing the soups to a full boil. (Add the tortellini and cook for 5 minutes. Roast the beet for the garnish.)

✱ Up to 1 month ahead, bake the cookies for Chocolate-Mint Ice Cream Sandwiches. Assemble the sandwiches, wrap, and freeze. At dessert time, remove them from the freezer; let stand 5 minutes.

✱ The day before your gathering, plan to shape the Checkerboard Rolls, cover, and chill until time to bake. Also cook the fennel and cauliflower for Fennel and Cauliflower Salad and make the salad dressing.

✱ To complete meal preparation, bake the rolls according to the recipe directions, and toss the salad.

are sure to spark conversations about cherished loved ones. They also help children become familiar with their ancestors and family they may not see often.

Before putting away family photos, use them to make fun labels for stockings. Or use current school photos or baby pictures for the kids' stockings.

Label the adults' stockings with their childhood photos. When crafting with photos, use color or black-and-white copies and save the originals.

With good food close at hand and the stage set for the holidays, 'tis the season for sitting back and enjoying the company of loved ones.

ABOVE: The holidays may be an indulgent time, but don't forget to cater to guests with lighter appetites. Couple Vegetable-Tortellini Soup (*front*) with another healthy favorite, Fennel and Cauliflower Salad (*back*) LEFT: Everyone loves ice cream, no matter the weather outside. Fill the freezer with make-ahead Chocolate-Mint Ice Cream Sandwiches so you're prepared when a craving strikes. For a Christmas touch, decorate the treats with crushed peppermint and spearmint candies.

Snowflake Pillow

Shown on *page 55* and *above*.

MATERIALS

½ yard of burlap

Snowflake-shape cookie cutters or
    stencil templates

1 piece of light green felt

Hole punch

Fabrics glue

White felt adhesive circles

Cotton embroidery floss and needle

Polyester fiberfill

Needle and sewing thread

INSTRUCTIONS

Cut two 16-inch squares from burlap.
Using the cookie cutter or template,
trace snowflake shapes onto the
light green felt; cut out. Use hole
punch to punch holes in the shapes
as desired.

Glue the snowflakes to the burlap;
tack at the centers. Attach white circles
to centers of snowflakes and small
circles to snowflake tips; embellish
with embroidery floss bows.

Pin the burlap squares together
with right sides facing. Sew around
the edges using a ½-inch seam
allowance; leave a hole for stuffing.
Turn the pillow right side out; press.
Stuff with polyester fiberfill and slip-
stitch the opening closed.

Stockings

Shown on *page 58* and *above*.

MATERIALS

Heavy cotton striped fabric

Rickrack trim in coordinating color

Buttons

Fabrics glue

Ribbons

Clothespins, vintage or new

Photocopies of family photos

Letter stickers and snowflake shapes

INSTRUCTIONS

Enlarge stocking pattern, *page 51*,
400%, using a photocopier. Use the
pattern to cut a stocking front and
back from striped fabric, reversing
one of the shapes. Cut a second
stocking front and back, varying the
look by changing the orientation of the
pattern. Fold the top edge of each
stocking piece under 1 inch toward
the wrong side; press.

Pin the right sides of the stocking
shapes together. Sew around the edges
using a ½-inch seam allowance, leaving the
top edge open. Clip the curves. Turn
the stocking right side out; press.

Trim the stockings as desired
with rickrack and buttons using
fabrics glue. Hang the stockings from
ribbons and clothespins. For extra
durability when the stockings are
stuffed, hang the stockings from the
ribbons, using the clothespin only as
decorative accessories.

Use a color or black-and-white
photocopy of a photo for the tag.
Decorate with letter stickers, snowflake shapes, rickrack, and buttons.
Clip the tags to the clothespins.

Chocolate-Mint Ice Cream Sandwiches

Shown on *page 60* and *above*.

Freeze the sandwiches before you
roll them into the crushed candy so
the candy will stick better and make
every bite a holiday delight.

½   cup butter

⅓   cup granulated sugar

¼   cup packed dark brown sugar

1½ teaspoons unsweetened
      cocoa powder

¼   teaspoon baking powder

1   egg

½   teaspoon vanilla

1½ ounces unsweetened
      chocolate, melted and slightly
      cooled

1¾ cups all-purpose flour

1   quart vanilla ice cream

Crushed peppermint or spearmint
      candies

Preheat oven to 350°F. In a large
mixing bowl, beat butter with an
electric mixer on medium to high
speed for 30 seconds. Beat in
granulated sugar, brown sugar, cocoa

powder, and baking powder until combined. Beat in egg and vanilla. Beat in melted chocolate.

Beat in as much flour as you can with the mixer. Stir in remaining flour with a wooden spoon. Cover and chill dough for 1 to 2 hours or until easy to handle.

On a lightly floured surface, roll dough ¼ inch thick. Using a 3-inch fluted round cutter or a 3×2-inch fluted diamond-shape cutter, cut out dough. Place cutouts on ungreased cookie sheet. Bake in the preheated oven for 7 to 8 minutes or until edges are firm. Transfer cookies to a wire rack. Cool completely.

Line a 2-quart rectangular baking dish with plastic wrap; set aside. Let ice cream stand for 10 minutes to soften slightly. Spread ice cream into prepared dish. Cover with plastic wrap and freeze until firm. Using the same cutters as used for cookies, cut ice cream into round or diamond shapes. Place ice cream cutouts on bottoms of half of the cookies. Top with remaining cookies, bottoms down. Place in the freezer to quickly refreeze sandwiches. Roll edges in crushed candies.

Wrap each sandwich in plastic wrap; freeze for 2 hours. Let stand at room temperature for 5 minutes before serving. Freeze for up to 1 month. Makes 6 sandwiches.

Vegetable-Tortellini Soup

Shown on *page 60* and *left*.

½   cup dry cannellini (white kidney) beans
4   cups water
Bouquet Garni
1   medium onion, chopped (½ cup)
3   cloves garlic, minced
1   tablespoon olive oil
3   cups chicken broth
8   ounces green beans, halved
½   of a fennel bulb, chopped (about ⅔ cup)
1   medium zucchini, chopped
2   medium tomatoes
2   sprigs fresh thyme
½   teaspoon salt
1   9-ounce package refrigerated spinach and cheese tortellini

Rinse beans; drain. In a large saucepan, combine beans and *2 cups* of the water. Bring to boiling; reduce heat. Simmer for 2 minutes. Remove from heat. Cover and let stand 1 hour. (Or, place beans in water in the saucepan. Cover; soak overnight in a cool place.) Drain. Rinse beans; set aside.

Prepare Bouquet Garni; set aside. In a 4-quart Dutch oven, cook onion and garlic in hot olive oil until tender. Add soaked beans and the remaining 2 cups water. Add Bouquet Garni and bring to boiling. Reduce heat; simmer, covered, for 55 minutes. Remove Bouquet Garni and discard.

Add chicken broth, green beans, fennel, zucchini, tomatoes, thyme, and salt. Bring to boiling; reduce heat. Simmer, covered, for 20 minutes. Add tortellini and simmer, covered, for 5 minutes more. Discard thyme sprigs. Ladle soup into bowls. Makes 4 to 5 servings.

Bouquet Garni: Cut a 10-inch square of 100-percent-cotton cheesecloth. Place 3 sprigs parsley, 2 bay leaves, ½ teaspoon whole black peppercorns, and 3 sprigs thyme on the cheesecloth. Draw up corners of square to create a bag and tie with clean kitchen string.

Smoked Sausage-Split Pea Soup

Shown on *page 59*.

Unlike other dry beans, split green peas do not require soaking, so you can ladle up this hearty, warming soup in less than 45 minutes.

1   small fennel bulb
4   cloves garlic, minced
1   tablespoon olive oil
1   medium onion, chopped (½ cup)
2   carrots, chopped
6   cups water
1¼ cups dry split green peas, rinsed and drained
½   teaspoon salt
¼   teaspoon freshly ground black pepper
6   ounces smoked sausage, cut into ½-inch slices
1   medium tomato, seeded and chopped
3   tablespoons red wine vinegar

Chop enough of the fennel bulb to measure 1 cup.

In a Dutch oven, cook garlic in hot oil over medium heat for 1 minute. Add onion and cook until golden brown. Add fennel and carrots; cook, stirring occasionally, until tender. Add water, split peas, salt, and pepper; bring to boiling. Reduce heat; simmer, uncovered, about 25 to 30 minutes or until split peas are tender.

Meanwhile, in a large skillet, brown sausage on all sides. Remove sausage from skillet using a slotted spoon; add sausage to soup along with tomato and red wine vinegar. Makes 5 to 6 servings.

Checkerboard Rolls

Shown on *page 59.*

Have all of the ingredients for the festive toppings ready before dipping the rolls into the melted butter because the butter will set up quickly.

2   tablespoons poppy seeds
2   tablespoons sesame seeds
1   teaspoon lemon-pepper
    seasoning
2   tablespoons yellow cornmeal
2   tablespoons grated or finely
    shredded Parmesan cheese
3   tablespoons butter, melted
16 1.3-ounce pieces frozen white
    roll dough

Grease a 9-inch square baking pan; set aside. In one shallow dish combine poppy seeds, sesame seeds, and lemon-pepper seasoning. In another shallow dish, combine cornmeal and Parmesan cheese. Place butter in a third dish. Working quickly, roll dough pieces in butter then in one of the seasoning blends to lightly coat. Coat half the rolls with one seasoning blend, and the remaining rolls with the other seasoning blend. Alternate rolls in prepared pan. Cover rolls with greased plastic wrap. Let thaw overnight in refrigerator.

Remove pan from refrigerator; uncover and let stand at room temperature for 45 minutes. (After 35 minutes, preheat oven to 375°F.)

Bake rolls in the preheated oven for 15 to 20 minutes or until golden. Cool slightly on a wire rack. Serve warm. Makes 16 rolls.

Winter White Vegetable Soup

Shown on *page 59.*

1   medium beet, trimmed
    (about 8 ounces)
1   large onion, chopped
    (1 cup)
1   tablespoon butter
1   small head cauliflower,
    coarsely chopped (4 cups)
2   medium turnips, peeled and
    cut into 1-inch pieces (3 cups)
2   medium potatoes, peeled and
    cut into 1-inch pieces (3 cups)
1   medium celeriac, peeled and
    cut into 1-inch pieces (3 cups)
1   large fennel bulb, sliced and
    leafy tops discarded (2 cups)
2   medium parsnips, peeled and
    coarsely chopped (1 cup)
2   cloves garlic, halved
¼   teaspoon salt
4   cups water
1½ cups milk
Milk
Snipped fresh chives (optional)

Preheat oven to 400°F. Wrap beet in foil. Roast in preheated oven about 1 hour or until just tender. Cool. Peel and chop beet; set aside.

Meanwhile, in a 4- to 5-quart Dutch oven cook onion in hot butter over medium heat about 5 minutes or until tender, stirring occasionally. Add cauliflower, turnips, potatoes, celeriac, fennel, parsnips, garlic, salt, and water. Bring to boiling; reduce heat. Simmer, covered, for 25 to 30 minutes or until vegetables are very tender. Remove from heat. Stir in 1½ cups milk. Let cool slightly, about 30 minutes.

Transfer soup mixture a little at a time to a blender or food processor; cover and blend or process until smooth. Return all soup mixture to Dutch oven. Add additional milk to obtain the desired consistency. Heat through. Ladle into individual bowls and sprinkle with beets. If desired, top with snipped chives. Makes 10 servings.

Fennel and Cauliflower Salad

Shown on *page 60.*

Fennel's mild flavor is similar to anise, a pleasing partner for cauliflower and fresh spinach.

2   medium fennel bulbs (about
    1 pound)
3   cups cauliflower florets
⅓   cup olive oil
⅓   cup white balsamic or white
    wine vinegar
2   tablespoons snipped fresh basil
1   clove garlic, minced
½   teaspoon anise seeds
¼   teaspoon salt
¼   teaspoon ground black
    pepper
4   to 5 cups fresh spinach leaves
2   cups cherry or grape
    tomatoes, halved
¼   cup finely shredded Parmesan
    cheese

Trim fennel; quarter lengthwise but do not remove core. Place fennel in a microwave-safe casserole. Add 2 tablespoons *water.* Cover and microwave on 100% power (high) for 5 to 7 minutes or until fennel is almost tender; drain. Cut into ¼- to ½-inch slices, discarding core.

Place cauliflower in a microwave-safe casserole. Add 2 tablespoons *water.* Cover and microwave on high about 4 minutes or until almost tender; drain. Cover; chill fennel and cauliflower for 2 to 24 hours.

Meanwhile, for dressing, in a small bowl, whisk together oil, vinegar, basil, garlic, anise seeds, salt, and pepper until smooth; set aside.

Line a large shallow bowl with spinach leaves. Spoon fennel and cauliflower over spinach. Add tomatoes. Drizzle vegetables with dressing and sprinkle with Parmesan cheese. Makes 8 to 10 servings.

tradition with a twist of lime

PHOTOGRAPHED BY **TRIA GIOVAN** WRITTEN BY **BECKY MOLLENKAMP**
FIELD EDITOR **SANDRA MOHLMANN**

Shana Smith drapes her Michigan
home in holiday spirit with a fresh, unexpected
combo of black, white, and lime green.

A Warm Welcome Holiday spirit begins at the front door, *opposite*. Shana Smith decks out her stoop with a large square wreath, fresh garland, and apple-filled urns. Apples also function as ornaments on a pair of pine trees that flank the steps.
Natural Touch Fresh greenery fills the Smith house with the scent of pine. The roses and paperwhites provide even more pleasant fragrance.

Shades of Winter Tall ceilings demand large-scale solutions. In the voluminous living room, a 15-foot Christmas tree with 47 strands of white lights fills a wide-open corner, *opposite*. A massive wreath-topped mirror sits on the mantel. The fresh greenery and chartreuse accessories add splashes of color to the white-walled space.

Pretty as a Package Fresh greenery and painted pinecones tied in polka-dot ribbon are elegant toppers for the Christmas presents, *left*.

Have a Ball Alive with color and texture, the Christmas tree includes a mix of black-and-white and chartreuse ornaments, *below*—a collection that took five years to amass. "I love ornaments that are a little bit on the funky side," Shana says.

As an interior designer, Shana Smith is adept at creating high style that is also livable and affordable. Her sensible, budget-savvy approach to decorating has her constantly thinking outside the box—a skill she puts to use when crafting her home's holiday decor.

Practicality motivated Shana to incorporate her home's existing color palette into her Christmas designs. There's no reason, she feels, to spend a fortune on new accessories that are only displayed for a few weeks. Her matter-of-fact philosophy frees her from the limitations of a traditional red-and-green Christmas palette.

"My husband, Matthew, and I don't have red or Christmas green in our house, so I don't use those colors for my holiday decorating," says the pragmatic designer.

Light-color walls, distressed white furniture, and neutral accents fill the Smith family's Michigan home. The potentially stark black-and-white palette is invigorated with drama from playful chartreuse green accents.

Black, white, and kicky green may be an unorthodox holiday color scheme, but Shana has no trouble making it work. She extends the palette throughout the house so it flows logically from room to room. Traditional touches meld with contemporary embellishments for a fresh twist on Christmas classics.

"I just wanted to create a timeless yet fresh design that was anything but boring and not over-the-top unrealistic," Shana says.

Converting her everyday decor into a seasonal showstopper takes Shana about a week. She starts the transformation with the tree. Vaulted ceilings in her living room call for a large tree—typically between 12 and 16 feet—that takes time to decorate.

Casual Elegance The dining room is the heart of holiday entertaining, *below.* To set the stage for casual gatherings, Shana covers her simple table with a no-frills burlap tablecloth and dresses the room with loads of fresh greenery and a few well-chosen accents in green and black-and-white.

Hung with Care The mantel may be the traditional hitching post for stockings, but Shana prefers to use her hearth for other decor. Instead, she hangs graphic-print stockings from a vintage ladder that rests against a wall near the Christmas tree, *left*.

On Display Every expanse of open wall space is an opportunity for Shana to expand on her holiday decor. This pretty tableau, *below*, includes a boxwood wreath hanging from an old window frame, fresh flowers, and an ornament-filled glass jar.

Adding 47 strands of white lights to the tree requires a full day. Shana lights each branch from the tip to the trunk and uses wire to secure the strands in place. Next she adds her growing collection of whimsical ornaments.

"I always start with one style and make sure they are evenly placed around the tree," she says. "Then I add the next style and the next." She then supplements the ornaments with large, dried hydrangea from her own garden. Each bloom is sprayed with adhesive and sprinkled with glitter before it's placed on the tree.

For another touch of the unexpected, Shana tops the tree with twigs and moss balls tied up in a big chartreuse satin bow. Shana says the overall look is reminiscent of a tree in Dr. Seuss's *How the Grinch Stole Christmas*. The funky Seuss-inspired look is repeated on the family's stockings, which feature large green polka dots, leopard-print banding, and pom-pom fringe. "I couldn't resist them," Shana says. "I'm a sucker for polka dots."

Shana finishes the living room's changeover by dressing up the mantel and banister with bows and "whatever else I have floating around that works," she says.

Finally, Shana gussies up the dining room and front stoop. In keeping with her color palette, she uses fresh limes and Granny Smith apples throughout the house, including on tabletop trees and in urns outside.

Shana's design ingenuity allows her to spend time and money on what really matters—making the holiday memorable for daughters Mackenzie and Quinn.

"Since I became a mom, the meaning of Christmas has changed," she says. "Nothing is more rewarding than watching your kids gasp with joy as they open their presents. They have no concept of money or wanting more, but as their mother, I want to give them everything and make it last all day."

deck the halls

Greens, poinsettias, and wreaths add to the cheer of the Christmas season. Check out this showy collection of both traditional and unique ideas.

fresh, fast & fabulous

Transform greenery, berries, and flowers into elegant holiday arrangements in minutes.

With just a little flair and our easy step-by-step directions, you can turn flowers and greenery into one-of-a-kind arrangements that lend a stylish, festive touch to your home for the holidays.

Talmage McLaurin, publisher of *Florists' Review* magazine, created these arrangements—and shows how to make them on *page 78*. The techniques are so clever yet so simple, that in no time you or your florist will come up with arrangements for holiday decorations that suit your home perfectly.

DESIGNED BY **TALMAGE MCLAURIN** WRITTEN BY **VERONICA FOWLER** PHOTOGRAPHED BY **GREG SCHEIDEMANN**

Great Ball of Fire

Add a contemporary touch to your holiday decor this season, *opposite*. This melon-size orb of glowing red carnations is easy to make: Simply place a ball of florist's foam atop a pretty glass cake plate and insert affordable flowers into the ball. For a luxurious upgrade, use roses.

Flames of Green

Take a pretty glass container, glue bits of greenery around it, and set candles inside to combine the freshness of greenery with the welcoming warmth of candlelight.

"I tried to come up with something that's *fun & pleasing* to look at but also something that's simple and not overly designed," McLaurin says.

Apple of Your Eye

Evoke holidays of old, when apples, oranges, and other fruits and nuts were used as yuletide decorations, with this simple arrangement, *opposite*. Start with a planter or vase, add a block of wet florist's foam and some greenery, and then fill in the arrangement with a few green apples for a finishing touch.

Vintage Beauty

Rummage around in the back of the cupboard or the attic for an interesting container to transform into this stylish accent, which is perfect for a side table, *right*. Here, an old silver trophy serves as a sophisticated perch for a florist's-foam ball covered in white carnations. Tendrils of ivy cascade down the sides of the trophy for an added touch of elegance.

Purely Ornamental

Create a new, inventive use for tree ornaments by turning them into delightful mini vases, *below*. For best results, choose mercury balls, which are more durable than glass balls, for this project. Remove the tops and set each ball into a pretty pot.

"After all, I think some of the best
arrangements are the *simple ones*,"
McLaurin says.

Bright Idea

Take a relaxing moment during the holiday rush to have some fun with this easy candlestick pair, perfect for displaying on a table, mantel, or any other spot around the home, *opposite*. Tuck pieces of wet florist's foam into two pots, add a bit of greenery and some hypericum berries (available from most florists), and finish off the pair with festive holiday-hue candles.

Bells upon Bells

Combine a few stems of lovely bells of Ireland with accents of silvery jingle bells to make a delightful miniature Christmas tree, *left*. Set the tree atop a silver goblet—whether a family heirloom or just an inexpensive look-alike—to achieve height and style.

Greenery with a Twist

Combine greenery and colorful carnations for a twist on classic holiday arrangements, *below*. Start by placing a piece of wet florist's foam in a waterproof cache pot (try silver or gold for added shimmer), insert flowers and fresh-cut greenery, and you're done.

Talmage McLaurin,

publisher of *Florists' Review* magazine, created these original designs. As a nationally recognized floral designer, he was inducted into the American Institute of Floral Design in 1988 and has presented four national symposium programs. His career in the industry began in a family-owned flower shop. He prefers simple centerpieces to the more complicated arrangements. "It's demystifying floral arranging," he says.

Great Ball of Fire & Vintage Beauty

The key to this fun centerpiece is the foam ball, which can be purchased for just a few dollars from a crafts store or a local florist. Soak the ball in tepid water until it is thoroughly saturated, and then insert carnations to completely cover the surface of the ball. You'll need 2 to 3 dozen carnations, depending on the size of the ball and the flowers.

Flames of Green

Prepare the glass surface by cleaning it with window cleaner. Then select any flat evergreen pieces you would like to use. Coat the greenery with spray adhesive.

Wait a few seconds for the adhesive to get tacky, and then attach each piece to the container with the ends hanging from the bottom of the container.

Allow the greenery to dry for a few minutes. Then trim the bottoms with sturdy scissors, floral snips, or garden shears.

Apple of Your Eye

Soak a block of florist's foam in tepid water. Position the foam in a planter or vase, and cut the foam so it's about one inch above the rim. Working in a clockwise fashion, tuck in sprigs of greenery, such as the bits of pine shown here.

Add another round of greenery. This time, you may wish to use something with a little contrast, such as the incense cedar with tiny golden berries shown here.

Insert florist's picks into apples. To keep the apples looking good through the holidays, dip the picks in cinnamon oil. It will act as an antiseptic to seal the punctures so the apples last longer—and it adds a festive scent.

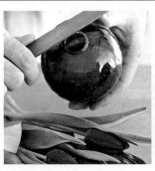

Purely Ornamental

Pull the hangers from the tops of the mercury balls and use a metal file to make the tops smooth.

Fill the balls with water. Add tulips or other flowers. If necessary, tuck in bits of bent greenery or twigs to hold the flowers upright.

Greenery with a Twist

Soak a block of florist's foam in tepid water, and then trim it with a knife so it fits into a waterproof pot or vase. Make a ring of greenery. Trim about a dozen carnations and insert them into the remaining foam, forming an even mound.

Bright Idea

Make pilot holes for florist's picks by drilling three or four holes into the base of each candle. Trim the picks as needed with garden shears.

Place a piece of wet florist's foam in a watertight cache pot, and cut off the foam at the rim. Make a ring of greenery and berries, leaving a space to insert the candle.

Bells upon Bells

A cone of florist's foam is key for creating this centerpiece. Soak the foam in tepid water until it's thoroughly saturated. Then cut a stem of bells of Ireland so the bits form lollipop-like shapes.

Insert the bells of Ireland pieces into the foam. This project will take about 12 stems cut into pieces.

Wrap chenille stems around the tiny loop at the back of each silver bell. Trim the chenille stems and insert each bell into the greenery. If desired, attach a bow to the base of the tree with florist's wire.

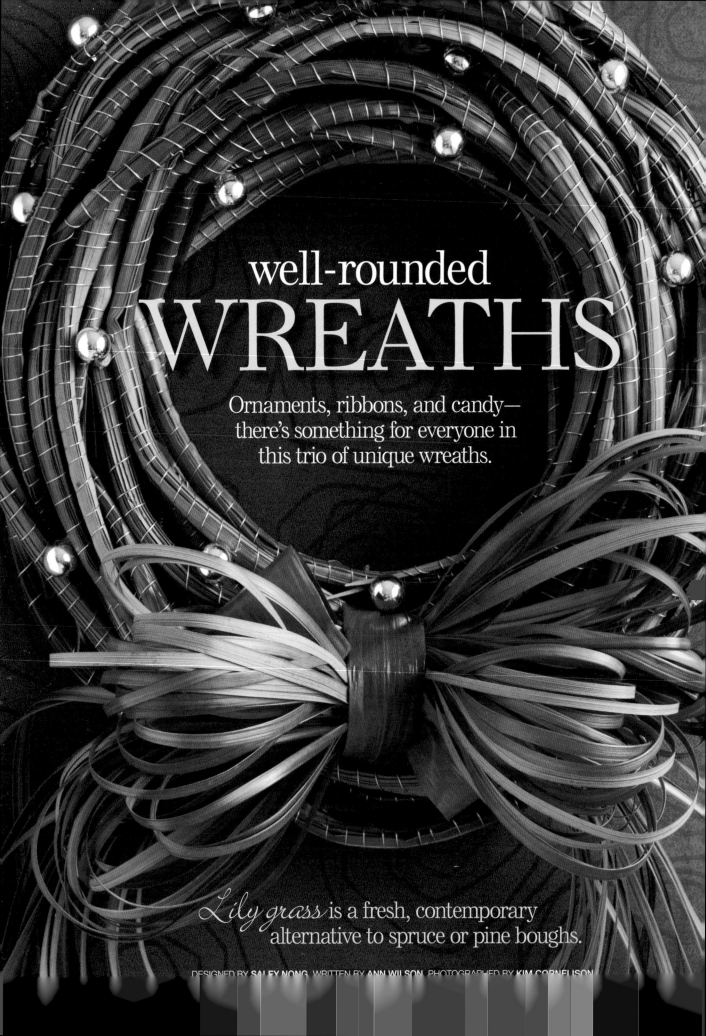

well-rounded
WREATHS

Ornaments, ribbons, and candy—
there's something for everyone in
this trio of unique wreaths.

Lily grass is a fresh, contemporary
alternative to spruce or pine boughs.

DESIGNED BY **SALLY NONG**. WRITTEN BY **ANN WILSON**. PHOTOGRAPHED BY **KIM CORNELISON**.

A *variation* on the theme: Float white ornaments on a frothy sea of light green ribbon.

Two-tone striped ribbon plays off the candy cane's iconic colors and pattern.

How-to instructions begin opposite.

we show you how!

Ribbon Wreath

MATERIALS

- Velvet, satin, and taffeta ribbon in shades of green
- Florist's wire
- Florist's picks
- Plastic-foam wreath form
- White ornaments
- Glue gun and hotmelt adhesive

INSTRUCTIONS

Cut lengths of velvet, satin, and taffeta ribbons. Fold the ribbon into loops, and wire several loops onto a florist's pick. Cover the surface of the plastic-foam wreath form with the ribbons, alternating ribbon types, shades, and heights for optimal interest. Nestle pearly white ornaments between the loops, and hot-glue them in place. Make the finishing bow by layering velvet ribbon loops onto a longer piece of ribbon and hot-gluing them in place. Wire the bow to a pick, and anchor it to the wreath bottom.

Lily Grass Wreath

MATERIALS

- Florist's-foam wreath form
- Chicken wire
- Lily grass
- Silver florist's wire
- Florist's pins
- Silver ornaments
- Banana leaf

INSTRUCTIONS

Soak a florist's-foam wreath form in water overnight; then wrap it with chicken wire. Wrap thin silver wire around bunches of lily grass. Stick one end of each bundle into the wet foam and wind the grass around the wreath, securing as needed with florist's pins. Twist and overlap the bundles for a loosely braided effect. Wire small silver ornaments in place; then shape a billowy bow from loops of lily grass cinched with a banana leaf. Wire the bow to the wreath bottom.

Candy-Cane Wreath

MATERIALS

- Plastic-foam wreath form
- White satin ribbon
- Glue gun and hotmelt adhesive
- Mini candy canes
- Small red ornaments
- Red and red-and-white striped ribbon

INSTRUCTIONS

Wrap a plastic-foam wreath form with white satin ribbon. Layer on the candy canes every which way, hot-gluing them in place. Hot-glue red ornaments atop the candy canes. Fashion a bow from three lengths of ribbon shaped into progressively smaller circles. Stack the ribbon circles, staple them at the center, wrap with another piece of ribbon around all three, and hot-glue a pair of tails to the back before affixing them to the bottom of the wreath with hot glue.

poinsettia
pointers

PRODUCED BY **KARIN LIDBECK-BRENT** WRITTEN BY **VERONICA FOWLER**
PHOTOGRAPHED BY **MICHAEL PARTENIO**

Say "Merry Christmas" loud and clear this year.
Use showy poinsettia blooms as cut flowers to enliven
all your holiday decorations.

Mass Appeal

Why settle for yet another poinsettia set out in a foil-covered pot? For a new look, set wet blocks of florist's foam on a row of trays. Then cut poinsettia flowers from the plant and insert them to cover the foam entirely, *this photo*. Figure about six flowers for every 12 inches of foam.

Simply Elegant

It's amazing the statement a single flower can make—and nothing is easier to display. Just trim off a poinsettia and lay it on the plate, *opposite*. Tie on a name tag to create a place card. To make the flower last a few days rather than a few hours, slip it into a water-filled vial, available at crafts stores and florist's shops. Wrap the vial in paper to conceal it, or leave it as is.

working poinsettias:

❋ Few, if any, florists carry poinsettias by the stem. Buy potted plants and cut them yourself. The branches are a bit delicate and tend to snap, so work carefully.

❋ When cut, poinsettias produce a milky sap. Set the stem in water for 30 minutes to allow the sap to wash away. Your flower will last up to two weeks this way.

❋ Be careful with the sap. It's a myth that poinsettias are poisonous, but the sap can irritate sensitive skin.

❋ The more water poinsettias get, the better. Surrounding the stem with as much moisture as possible will help it last longer. Poinsettias in a vase with their stems submerged almost up to their necks are likely to last up to two weeks longer than ones with just a couple of inches of stem inserted into wet florist's foam.

Peppered with Berries
Pepper berries, available from florists, look wonderful when interspersed with poinsettias.

Branching Out
Create a tree that reflects the spare beauty of winter by cutting several long branches from trees and shrubs, *above*. Arrange the branches in a large urn or other container, anchoring them with blocks of foam or pebbles.

Remove the hanger top from an ornament so it's open. Cut two 7-inch lengths of ⅛-inch ribbon, and glue the ends of the ribbon pieces to the sides of the opening so they can be tied and used to hang the ornament from the branch. Use a quick, fast-drying waterproof adhesive.

Set the ball atop a small drinking glass to hold it steady and fill the bottom fourth of it with water; insert the poinsettia. Tie it onto the tree.

Good Cheer

Put julep cups, goblets, small trophies, and any other silver containers you may have around the house to good use by tucking a cut poinsettia or two into each one, *right*. They're especially pretty as a collection along a mantel (as long as it's not above a real fireplace that produces leaf-destroying heat). Don't have any heirloom silver around? Take a can of chrome spray paint and turn inexpensive containers into look-alikes.

Nature's Own Ornament

Poinsettias are a naturally showy way to enliven a Christmas tree. Insert them into small floral vials filled with water. (You may want to enlarge the vial opening with a pencil first so no delicate stems snap.)

Here, they've been tucked into a 3-foot Canadian spruce, *below*. With trees that have dense, tight foliage, such as spruce and balsam, you can get away with simply tucking the vials into the foliage. For trees with looser foliage, such as pine, wire the vials to branches with florist's wire. Check water levels daily.

buying poinsettias:

A poinsettia is a poinsettia is a poinsettia. Whether you buy it at a discount supermarket or an upscale florist's shop, if it looks healthy and happy, it is. If it's at all droopy, don't buy it. Once a poinsettia wilts, it doesn't revive.

❊ Choose plants that have leaves all the way to the soil line. If the plant is a little bare on the bottom, it's likely stressed and has been dropping leaves.

❊ Check the true flowers, which are tiny and budlike and are located at the bases of the big, colorful modified leaves (called bracts) that most people think are the flowers. Ideally, the true flowers should be green- or red-tipped, which means the plant is less developed. If the flowers have yellow pollen on them, the plant won't last as long.

❊ Look for variations. Poinsettias come in all sorts of wonderful colors, including cream, mottled or marbled pinks and peaches, peppermint-like swirls, plum colors, and greenish-whites. Miniature poinsettias, just inches high, also are fun.

❊ Poinsettias are extremely temperature sensitive. If it's less than 50 degrees outside, wrap the entire plant in plastic or paper to protect it while you bring it home. Once you're home, keep it away from icy drafts as well as heat vents and fireplaces.

❊ Poinsettias in pots need to be kept lightly but evenly watered. Keep them too soggy and they'll drop leaves. If they're too dry, they'll wilt and won't recover.

nature's tree

Add magic to the table with an all-white feather tree. Subtle additions—ornaments fashioned from dried orange slices and pinecones of varying shapes and sizes—allow the simplicity of the ivory tree to shine.

holiday harvest

Savor the spirit of the season with pretty dressings **inspired by nature.** Pinecones, kumquats, and greenery lend a warm-and-cozy mood to holiday decor.

DESIGNED BY: KAREN LIDBECK-BRENT   PHOTOGRAPHED BY: MICHAEL PARTENIO   WRITTEN BY: BECKY MOLLENKAMP

Extend the *warm colors* and elements of autumn into the Christmas season.

striking centerpiece

Bright and bold, this eye-pleasing centerpiece grabs attention. Fill a glass hurricane container with kumquats and top with a pinecone-shape candle and a few evergreen sprigs.

bountiful baskets

Seasonal selections turn a trio of simple baskets into a hearty display that's a treat to behold. Arrange clove-studded oranges, kumquats, pinecones, evergreen branches, and seeded eucalyptus in three baskets. Then stack them neatly and place a candle on top.

festive harvest

Combine backyard finds with fruit
and elegant roses to create a bountiful
display that's perfect for the season—
and an economical alternative to an
all-flower arrangement. Large
pinecones, clove-studded oranges,
kumquats, seeded eucalyptus, and
sprays of wheat burst from the basket.
A few soft-hue roses finish the look.

A *neutral color palette* wraps the home in serenity for the season.

welcoming wreath

A simply chic wreath of pinecones and kumquats adds a graphic flourish to the mantel or door. Glue neat rows of white spruce pinecones and kumquats to a green moss wreath and top off with a large satin bow.

INSTRUCTIONS BEGIN ON PAGE 94.

1

2

1. Nature's Tree

MATERIALS

- Oranges
- Pinecones from 1 to 6 inches
- Florist's wire
- Kumquats
- Feather tree

INSTRUCTIONS

Cut oranges into very thin slices. Lay the slices on a baking sheet and place in an oven set on the lowest temperature (125°F to 200°F) for six hours. Remove oranges from the oven when the slices have only a slight amount of moisture left and are still orange in color. Lay the dried orange slices on paper towels overnight to absorb any extra moisture.

Sort the pinecones by size from largest to smallest. Thread wire

through the top of the pinecones and wire them to the tree with the largest cones on the bottom branches. Trim the wire ends. Continue wiring the pinecones to the tree in order by size.

Push a short length of wire through each orange slice and kumquat. Wire the fruit to the tree, and trim the wire ends.

2. Bountiful Baskets

MATERIALS

- 12-inch square basket
- 11-inch round basket
- 9-inch round basket
- Florist's foam for artificial arrangements
- Glue gun and hotmelt adhesive

- 10 to 12 juice oranges, whole cloves, kumquats
- Pinecones in assorted sizes from 1 to 6 inches
- Wooden florist's picks
- Assorted greenery
- Seeded eucalyptus
- Small pillar candle and holder

INSTRUCTIONS

Choose three baskets that will stack with the largest on the bottom to the smallest on top. Cut blocks of florist's foam to fill each basket. For the center of the largest basket, cut a circular piece of foam the size of the medium-size-basket bottom and an inch higher than the largest basket's sides. (A) Place the foam in the large basket and then glue it to

A

B

the bottom of the medium-size basket. This will raise the medium-size basket higher than the outside edge of the largest basket. Repeat for the small basket.

Stud the oranges with cloves in a variety of patterns. Insert florist's picks into the studded oranges and kumquats. Wire florist's picks to the pinecones.

(B) Fill the baskets with oranges, kumquats, pinecones, greenery, and seeded eucalyptus. Nestle a small pillar candle in the top basket.

3. Festive Harvest

MATERIALS

- Ceramic or resin waterproof basket
- Florist's foam for fresh arrangements
- Seeded eucalyptus, roses, wheat spikes, kumquats, oranges, whole cloves
- Florist's wire
- Pinecones in assorted sizes from 2 to 6 inches
- Florist's picks

INSTRUCTIONS

Cut the foam to size for your container. Soak the foam in water according to the manufacturer's instructions. Press the foam into the container. Wire 4 to 6 spikes of wheat together with florist's wire.

Press cloves into the oranges. Insert florist's picks into the oranges and kumquats. Wire the picks to the pinecones.

Insert pinecones into the container to establish the overall shape of your arrangement. Add the wheat bundles, roses, oranges, and kumquats. Tuck in small pieces of seeded eucalyptus to finish.

4. Welcoming Wreath

MATERIALS

- White spruce pinecones from 1 to 2 inches
- Kumquats
- Glue gun and hotmelt adhesive
- 13-inch-diameter moss wreath
- Wide ribbon

INSTRUCTIONS

Sort the pinecones and kumquats by size from largest to smallest. Glue a row of pinecones to the wreath with the largest pinecones on the outer area of the wreath. Repeat the process with a row of kumquats followed by a row of pinecones until the wreath is covered. Tie a ribbon bow, and glue it to the top of the wreath.

outdoor
decor

During the holidays, festive decorative touches placed outside make family and friends feel welcome even before they cross your threshold. With a few items from the store—and a little imagination—you can create your own unique outdoor holiday decorations.

PRODUCED AND WRITTEN BY **RICHARD KOLLATH** AND **ED McCANN**
PHOTOGRAPHED BY **MATTHEW BENSON**

Natural Spheres

Large grapevine spheres wrapped with miniature white lights make a modern and dramatic statement, *left*. Brown corded lights disappear against the grapevine; anchor the plug end of the light strand to the sphere with wire; then wrap as you would a yarn ball, adding more sets of lights as desired. **TIP:** *Make sure the lights you choose are rated for outdoor use.*

Through the Grapevine

Grapevine trees wrapped in miniature white lights flank an entry door, adding holiday sparkle to the front porch, *opposite*. As with the spheres, brown corded lights are almost invisible against the brown vines. The trees are anchored with wooden plant stakes stuck in foam wedged into the planter pots. **TIP:** *Conceal the foam base with sheet moss.*

Snowballs

This mound of shimmering prelit spheres stacked in an urn, *right*, looks like snowballs just waiting to be thrown. Plug the spheres into a power strip hidden inside the urn, and then accent them with boxwood greenery. **TIP:** *A strand of monofilament wrapped around the spheres keeps the stack secure.*

Fresh greenery is a natural backdrop for your outdoor holiday decorating.

Standard Greeting

Make this welcoming holiday topiary by inserting boxwood greenery in a foam sphere and adding fresh or faux winterberry sprays for a vibrant pop of red, *left*. Anchor the branch trunk in foam tucked inside a sturdy pot; secure the top to the trunk using firm downward pressure. **TIP:** *Cutting the branch end at a sharp angle makes it easier to drive and anchor in the foam.*

Basket of Cheer

A wire basket filled with greenery and large ornaments, *below*, makes a simple and festive holiday welcome on a porch or near your front door. For a variation on the multicolor scheme here, you can use balls in a single hue. Or, instead, tuck greenery among ornaments arranged in a wicker basket, a wooden box, or a large clay flowerpot. **TIP:** *Painted ornaments may lose their finish if left out in the rain or snow.*

Glowing Stars

Illuminated stars lead guests to your front door and make a sophisticated and beautiful holiday decorating statement, *opposite*. Here, traditional plastic Moravian stars in two different sizes are arranged on a bench covered with cedar branches and California sugar pinecones. **TIP:** *A concealed power strip wired to the back of the bench eliminates unsightly cords and plugs; a gray extension cord runs discreetly to an outside outlet.*

Christmas treats

Whether you enjoy sending sweet season's greetings to friends and family or you prefer to indulge in the treats yourself, you'll love this collection of Christmas recipes and food-gift ideas.

sweet tidings

LUSCIOUS TREATS in shades of cream and
white set the mood for a **WHITE CHRISTMAS,**
even if there isn't a **SNOWFLAKE** around for miles.

Written by LINDA HENRY   Food stylist CHARLES WORTHINGTON   Photographed by PETE KRUMHARDT

TAKE THE CAKE Dinner will end with a flourish when you serve this lavish White-on-White Cheesecake. Dress it for the season by wrapping a silky ribbon around the crust; secure with a dollop of white icing. Mound shaved white chocolate curls and pink-and-white sugar-sprinkled stars on top.

SWEETS STICKS Try a new shape for shortbread by cutting the dough into cookie sticks, *opposite left*. Serve the bite-size Shortbread Sticks in a white decorative vase for a snowy finish.

SUGAR AND SPICE Underneath a rich layer of velvety Buttercream Frosting lies a tender, cinnamon-flavored cake, *opposite right*. For a crowning touch, top the Cinnamon-Apple Spice Cake with a few sugar cookies shaped and frosted to look like Christmas ornaments.

YUMMY SUGARY SWEETS WILL BRING A
smile to every face, YOUNG OR OLD.

SPIRITED LATTE Ready in a few minutes, Eggnog Latte, *above left,* is the perfect drink to whip up for unexpected guests. So sip to your heart's content because this new twist on eggnog will warm holiday spirits.

TREE TREATS Create this Tiered Meringue Tree fantasy, *above right,* for hungry nibblers by piling mini-meringue confections high.

ICY COLD GOODNESS These Shimmering Icicle Cookies, *far left,* are designed for December indulgence. Eat the sparkly treats, or hang them with ribbons from tree branches.

OH, FUDGE! This Heavenly Key Lime Fudge, *left,* can only lead to one thing ... compliments.

TIERED MERINGUE TREE

Shown *above* and on *page 104.*

    3   egg whites
    1   teaspoon vanilla
    ¼   teaspoon cream of tartar
    ¼   teaspoon peppermint
        extract
    1½ cups sugar
        Pink Icing

Preheat oven to 300°F. In a large mixing bowl, beat egg whites, vanilla, cream of tartar, and extract with an electric mixer on high speed until soft peaks form (tips curl). Add the sugar, 1 tablespoon at a time, beating until stiff peaks form (tips stand straight). Spoon this meringue into a large pastry bag fitted with a large star tip. Pipe small mounds (about 1 inch in diameter) 1 inch apart onto lightly greased baking sheets. (You should have about 130 meringue stars total.)

Bake meringues about 20 minutes or until firm and bottoms are very lightly browned. Transfer to racks; cool. Spread bottoms of half of meringue stars with about 1 teaspoon Pink Icing. Gently press bottom sides of remaining meringue stars into icing to form sandwiches.

Dot icing in an 8-inch circle on a flat serving plate. Build the tree's first layer by arranging a circle of 15 meringue sandwiches on their sides with points of one side of each sandwich facing the edge of plate. Within this circle, make a circle of 10 sandwiches.

On this foundation, stack ever-smaller circles of sandwiches on their sides to form a tree or cone shape. Use small amounts (about ½ teaspoon) of icing to attach each sandwich to the previous layer, forming 5 to 6 layers of meringue sandwiches (25 in first layer, 15 in the second, then 13, 7, 4, and 1 in the consecutive layers that follow). Makes 65 meringue sandwiches.

Pink Icing: Combine 3 cups sifted *powdered sugar,* 3 tablespoons softened *butter,* and 1½ teaspoons *vanilla.* Add 1 or 2 drops *red food coloring* to tint a light-pink color. Stir in ¼ cup finely chopped *candied red cherries.* Stir in 1 to 2 tablespoons *milk* until icing is smooth and of spreading consistency.

WHITE-ON-WHITE CHEESECAKE

Shown *above* and on *page 103.*

    ½   cup butter, softened
    ¼   cup packed brown sugar
    4   eggs
    1¼ cups all-purpose flour
    4   8-ounce packages cream
        cheese, softened
    1¼ cups granulated sugar
    ¼   cup all-purpose flour
    4   teaspoons vanilla
    2   8-ounce cartons dairy
        sour cream
    ¼   cup granulated sugar

Preheat oven to 350°F. In a large mixing bowl, beat butter for 30 seconds. Add brown sugar; beat until fluffy. Add 1 of the eggs; beat well. Slowly beat in the 1¼ cups flour until combined. Divide dough in half. Cover and refrigerate 1 portion.

Spread remaining portion onto the bottom of an ungreased 10-inch springform pan with sides removed. Place on baking sheet. Bake for 10 minutes. Remove from oven; cool completely.

When bottom crust has cooled, attach sides of pan. Press chilled dough portion onto sides to a height of about 1¾ inches. Set aside.

Increase oven temperature to 450°F. In a large mixing bowl, beat cream cheese and the 1¼ cups granulated sugar until fluffy. Beat in the ¼ cup flour at low speed until smooth. Add the remaining 3 eggs and 3 teaspoons of the vanilla all at once, beating at low speed until just combined. Stir in ½ cup of the sour cream. Pour batter into the crust-lined pan. Place in a shallow baking pan in oven.

Bake for 10 minutes. Reduce oven temperature to 300°F. Bake 30 minutes more or until center appears nearly set when gently shaken. Remove from oven. Stir together remaining sour cream, the ¼ cup granulated sugar, and the remaining 1 teaspoon vanilla. Spread mixture evenly over top of cheesecake. Return to oven; bake 15 minutes more.

Remove from oven. Cool on wire rack for 15 minutes. Loosen crust from sides of pan. Cool for 30 minutes more. Remove sides of pan; cool completely. Cover and chill overnight or at least 4 hours. Before slicing, let stand at room temperature for 15 minutes. Garnish with white chocolate curls and star cutouts if desired. Makes 16 servings.

SHORTBREAD STICKS

Shown *opposite, top right* and on *page 102.*

1½ cups all-purpose flour
½ cup sifted powdered sugar
⅔ cup butter
2 tablespoons finely chopped candied ginger
¼ cup finely chopped sliced almonds
¼ cup candied red cherries, finely chopped
1 tablespoon granulated sugar

Preheat oven to 325°F. Combine flour and powdered sugar. Cut in butter until mixture resembles fine crumbs and starts to cling. Stir in ginger. Form into a ball; knead gently until smooth. On a lightly floured surface, roll dough into a 14×6-inch rectangle (about ¼ inch thick).

Combine almonds, cherries, and granulated sugar. Sprinkle evenly over dough; press in lightly. Using a knife, cut into twenty 6×½-inch strips. Place about ½ inch apart on an ungreased cookie sheet.

Bake about 18 minutes or until bottoms just start to brown. Cool on cookie sheet 5 minutes. Transfer to wire racks; cool. Makes about 20 sticks.

SHIMMERING ICICLE COOKIES

Shown *opposite, bottom right* and on *page 104.*

¾ cup butter, softened
¾ cup granulated sugar
¼ teaspoon baking powder
1 egg
½ teaspoon vanilla
¼ teaspoon almond extract
2 cups all-purpose flour
Powdered Sugar Icing
White edible glitter or coarse sugar

In a large mixing bowl, beat butter with an electric mixer for 30 seconds. Add granulated sugar and baking powder. Beat until combined. Beat in egg, vanilla, and almond extract until combined. Beat in as much of the flour as you can with the mixer. Stir in any remaining flour. Cover; chill dough about 1 hour or until easy to handle.

Preheat oven to 375°F. On a lightly floured surface, shape about ½ tablespoon of dough into a 5-inch rope, tapering the end. Repeat with another ½ tablespoon of dough. Place ropes side by side and twist together. If desired, poke a small hole in the top of each cookie using a drinking straw.

Place cookies about 1 inch apart on an ungreased cookie sheet. Bake for 8 to 10 minutes or until edges are firm and bottoms are lightly browned. Cool on cookie sheet 1 minute. Transfer to wire racks; cool.

Brush Powdered Sugar Icing over each cookie; sprinkle with glitter. Makes 24 cookies.

Powdered Sugar Icing: Stir together 1 cup sifted *powdered sugar,* 1 tablespoon *milk,* and ¼ teaspoon *almond extract.* Stir in additional *milk,* 1 teaspoon at a time, to make icing smooth and of brushing consistency.

EGGNOG LATTE

Shown on *page 104.*

2 cups dairy eggnog
1 tablespoon light-color rum
1 tablespoon bourbon
1 cup hot brewed espresso
White nonpareils
White candy canes (optional)

In a small heavy saucepan, heat eggnog over medium heat until hot (do not boil). In the meantime, stir rum and bourbon into hot espresso.

Transfer about *half* of the eggnog and *half* of the espresso mixture to a blender container. Cover and blend until very frothy. Repeat with remaining eggnog and remaining espresso mixture. Divide latte evenly among coffee cups. Sprinkle with nonpareils. Serve with a white candy cane if desired. Makes 5 (6- to 8-ounce) servings.

HEAVENLY KEY LIME FUDGE

Shown *opposite, top left* and on *page 104.*

If you wish, you can substitute fresh Key lime juice or regular lime juice for the bottled juice.

3 cups white baking pieces
1 14-ounce can (1¼ cups) sweetened condensed milk
2 teaspoons finely shredded lime peel
2 tablespoons bottled Key lime juice or regular lime juice
1 cup chopped macadamia nuts, toasted if desired

Line an 8×8×2-inch baking pan with foil, extending foil over edges of pan. Butter foil; set aside.

In a large heavy saucepan, cook and stir baking pieces and sweetened condensed milk over low heat just until pieces are melted and mixture is smooth. Remove from heat. Stir in lime peel and lime juice. Stir in nuts.

Spread mixture evenly in prepared pan. Cover and chill about 2 hours or until set.

Lift fudge from pan using edges of foil. Peel off foil; cut into pieces. Store in an airtight container at room temperature for up to 1 week or in the freezer for up to 2 months. Makes 2½ pounds of fudge.

CINNAMON-APPLE SPICE CAKE

Shown *bottom left* and on *page 102.*

- 1 14- to 14½-ounce jar spiced apple rings
- 2 cups all-purpose flour
- 1½ teaspoons baking powder
- 1 teaspoon ground cinnamon
- ½ teaspoon baking soda
- ½ teaspoon salt
- ½ cup butter, softened
- 1¼ cups sugar
- 1 teaspoon vanilla
- 3 eggs
- ¾ cup buttermilk
    Buttercream Frosting

Preheat oven to 350°F. Grease and lightly flour two 8×8×2-inch square baking pans; set pans aside.

Drain apple rings; discard syrup. Place apples in a food processor bowl or blender container. Cover and process or blend until almost smooth (should have ¾ cup). Set aside. Stir together flour, baking powder, cinnamon, soda, and salt; set aside.

In a bowl, beat butter with an electric mixer for 30 seconds. Add sugar and vanilla; beat until combined. Add eggs, one at a time, beating well. Add flour mixture and buttermilk alternately to beaten mixture, beating on

low speed after each addition just until combined. Fold in processed apples. Divide batter evenly between prepared pans. Bake for 25 to 30 minutes or until a wooden toothpick inserted near center comes out clean.

Cool in pans on racks for 10 minutes. Remove from pans; cool. Frost with Buttercream Frosting. Makes 12 to 16 servings.

Buttercream Frosting: In a mixing bowl, beat ½ cup *butter* with an electric mixer until fluffy. Gradually add 3 cups sifted *powdered sugar,* beating well on low speed. Slowly beat in ⅓ cup *milk* and 2 teaspoons *vanilla.* Gradually beat in 3½ cups sifted *powdered sugar.* If necessary, beat in additional *milk* to make frosting easy to spread.

santas' favorite

In a season of traditions, a classic recipe deserves a spot on the menu. Chocolate-chunk cookies come as no surprise to an anticipating tongue, but add to the original by including cocoa powder in the mix or by dipping the cookies in a rich chocolate ganache for a tasty twist. To travel with the treats (or to give them as a gift), cover a craft box with bold papers—you can enhance them using decorative-edge scissors—and encircle the box top with satin ribbon.

Written by **Katherine C. Nugent** Photographed by **Greg Scheidemann** Food stylist **Janet Pittman**

simple sweets

Get out of the kitchen and **INTO THE CONVERSATION** when you're playing hostess this holiday season. **DELICIOUS DESSERTS** made for many can be simple without tasting that way. Try playing with a chic Christmas color scheme—**RICH BROWNS COUPLED WITH WINTER WHITES AND PRETTY PINKS**—for a display that will inspire admiring "oohs" and "aahs."

just desserts

The tart taste of orange liqueur calms the sweetness of the chocolate in this fudge brownie. It takes 30 minutes to bake, so you can prepare the glaze while you wait. Use your time wisely and you also can complete this four-ingredient coffee milk shake before the brownie is baked. For an appealing accent, prepare snowflake-dotted chocolate shards (see page 113 for instructions) the night before, and submerse one in your after-dinner shake.

all balled up

Inside these no-bake treats is a base of unconventional ingredients, such as coffee crystals and dried cherries. Dipped and drizzled in melted chocolate (see page 113 for instructions), the sweets are as close as it gets to too much of a good thing. For an easy display, tip the corners of a napkin with crystal beads. Tie a knot at the end of nylon beading thread, string on the beads, and then stitch the embellishment to a napkin.

layer it on

This sinfully easy four-layer torte holds the surprisingly light and sweet taste of blackberries. The secret? It's made from a purchased mix and the blackberry puree is fresh berries blended with jam. Top the cake with icing and make-ahead pink-and-white chocolate curls (see page 113 for instructions). For extra sparkle, spell out holiday sentiments with letter charms and dangle them from your serving platter.

chocolate *secrets*

DELICATE CURLS: In a small saucepan, melt 1 cup white vanilla-flavor candy-coating pieces and 1 tablespoon shortening until smooth. In another small saucepan, melt 1 cup pink vanilla-flavor candy-coating pieces and 1 tablespoon shortening until smooth. Using a double thickness of foil, form a 1×2×1-inch bar-shape container. Alternately spoon each color of melted candy into the container to create a ½-inch-thick bar. Use a knife to swirl the mixture. Let stand in a cool, dry place until the chocolate is firm; then carefully peel the foil away from the candy.

To make the curls, let the marbled bar come to room temperature; then carefully draw a vegetable peeler across the bar. For small curls, use the thin side of the bar; for large curls, use the broad surface.

PRETTY PIPES: Place melted pink or red vanilla-flavor candy coating in a disposable decorating bag. Cut a small hole in the corner, and pipe or drizzle small designs onto coated candies. Let the candies stand in a cool, dry place until piped design is firm.

SHAPELY SHARDS: Pipe melted white and pink vanilla-flavor candy-coating pieces onto a baking sheet lined with waxed paper; pipe a random arrangement of snowflakes over the entire surface. When it's firm, spread melted chocolate-flavor candy coating (cooled) over the top of the piped lines ⅛ inch thick. Let stand in a cool, dry place until chocolate is firm; then carefully peel the chocolate away from the waxed paper. Break or cut the chocolate into irregular-shape shards. Cover and chill in refrigerator until needed.

MELTING CHOCOLATE: To melt chocolate or candy coating for spreading or dipping, there's no need for a double boiler. Use a deep, heavy saucepan and add shortening if directed in recipe. Melt chocolate or candy coating and shortening over low heat, stirring constantly. Or place chocolate or candy coating (and shortening if directed) in a microwave-safe measuring cup and melt in a microwave oven on 100 percent power (high) for 60 seconds for each 3-ounce measure until chocolate is just soft enough to stir smoothly. (The chocolate pieces will not appear melted until stirred.)

STORING CHOCOLATE:
• Chocolate must be stored below 70°F, which means in the refrigerator or freezer, especially in the summer. It has to be tightly wrapped or stored in an airtight container.
• When you take it out of the fridge, leave it in its wrapping until it's at room temperature. Water condensing on the surface can cause problems in melting and cooking.
• Dark-chocolate candy will keep in the refrigerator for up to one year; milk chocolate will keep six months. All chocolate will keep in the freezer for up to one year.

SEND SOMETHING SWEET: Go ahead—make someone's holiday! Send them a package of the cookie assortment pictured on *page 108*. For safe sending, line the box with plastic or foil before packing it with cookies. Fit the gift box snugly into a sturdy box for mailing. Use strapping tape to seal the box shut, and mark the box "perishable." ❊

For more ideas: www.bhg.com/sipchocolate

Cherry-Rum Nut Balls

Shown on *page 111.*

Try a fun way to pretty up these candy-coated gems. Drizzle them with melted pink or red vanilla-flavor candy coating. (See directions, page 113.)

- ¾ cup chopped dried tart cherries
- ¼ cup dark rum
- 2 cups finely crushed vanilla wafers (about 54)
- ¾ cup ground pecans, almonds, or walnuts
- ¼ cup powdered sugar
- ¼ cup butter, melted
- 2 tablespoons frozen orange juice concentrate, thawed
- 1⅔ cups white baking pieces
- 2 tablespoons shortening

In a small bowl, combine cherries and rum; cover and let stand for 1 hour. Line two baking sheets with waxed paper; set aside.

In a large mixing bowl, combine crushed vanilla wafers, ground pecans, and powdered sugar. Add undrained cherry mixture, melted butter, and orange juice concentrate; stir until combined. Shape mixture into 1-inch balls. Place balls on prepared baking sheets; let stand until dry (about 1 hour).

In a small, heavy saucepan, combine baking pieces and shortening. Cook and stir over medium-low heat until melted. Remove from heat. Dip rum balls in the mixture, turning each one to coat completely. Remove each ball with a fork and return to baking sheets. Drizzle with any remaining melted mixture. Chill in the refrigerator for 15 minutes or until coating is set. Makes about 45.

To store: Place balls in layers separated by waxed paper in an airtight container; cover. Store in refrigerator for up to 1 month. Do not freeze.

Chocolate-Chunk Cookies

Shown on *page 108.*

To set the melted chocolate on the cookies quickly, place the dipped cookies on a baking sheet lined with waxed paper and refrigerate about 5 minutes.

- 1 cup butter, softened
- ¾ cup granulated sugar
- ¾ cup packed brown sugar
- 1 teaspoon baking soda
- 1 egg
- 1 teaspoon vanilla
- 2½ cups all-purpose flour
- 11 to 12 ounces white baking chips and/or semisweet chocolate, chopped

White Chocolate Coating (optional)
Chocolate Coating (optional)

Preheat oven to 375°F. In a large mixing bowl, beat the butter with an electric mixer on medium to high speed for 30 seconds. Add granulated sugar, brown sugar, and baking soda; beat until well combined. Add egg and vanilla; beat well. Gradually beat in flour. Stir in the white baking chips and/or the chopped semisweet chocolate chunks.

Drop rounded teaspoons of dough 2 inches apart onto ungreased cookie sheets. Bake in the preheated oven for 8 to 10 minutes or until edges are lightly browned. Transfer to wire racks and let cool.

If desired, dip half of each cookie into the White Chocolate Coating or Chocolate Coating; place on waxed paper and let stand for 30 minutes or until set. Makes 48.

Double-Chocolate-Chunk Cookies: Prepare recipe as above, except use 2 eggs. Add 2 ounces unsweetened chocolate, melted and cooled, to the egg mixture. Reduce flour to 2 cups and add ½ cup unsweetened cocoa powder. Stir in white baking chips and/or chopped semisweet chocolate.

White Chocolate Coating: In a small heavy saucepan, combine 2 cups white baking pieces and 3 tablespoons shortening. Cook and stir over medium-low heat until chocolate is melted. Cool slightly.

Chocolate Coating: In a small heavy saucepan, combine 2 cups semisweet chocolate pieces and 3 tablespoons shortening. Cook and stir over medium-low heat until chocolate is melted. Cool slightly.

Chocolate-Blackberry Torte

Shown on *page 112.*

Use cake mix to streamline the preparation of this decadent dessert.

- Nonstick cooking spray
- 2½ cups fresh blackberries or frozen blackberries, thawed
- 1 2-layer-size dark chocolate cake mix
- 1½ cups blackberry jam
- 2 cups whipping cream
- ⅔ cup dairy sour cream
- ¼ cup sifted powdered sugar
- 1 teaspoon vanilla
- Marbled Pink-and-White Chocolate Curls (See directions, page 113.)

Preheat oven to 350°F. Lightly coat two 9×1½-inch round baking pans with nonstick cooking spray. Line bottoms with parchment paper or waxed paper; lightly coat paper with nonstick cooking spray. Set aside.

Place blackberries in a blender or food processor. Cover and blend or process until smooth. Strain berries through a fine-mesh sieve (you should have about 1 cup puree); discard seeds. Set puree aside.

In a large mixing bowl, prepare cake mix according to package directions, reducing water to ½ cup. Stir in berry puree. Divide batter between the prepared pans.

Bake in the preheated oven about 35 minutes or until wooden toothpicks inserted near the centers come out clean. Cool cakes in pans for 10 minutes. Remove from pans; remove waxed paper or parchment. Cool completely on wire racks.

To assemble, using a serrated knife, carefully slice each cake layer in half horizontally, making four layers. Place the first layer on a large serving plate. Spread *½ cup* jam on top of the cake layer. Repeat with two cake layers and remaining jam. Top with remaining cake layer.

For frosting, in a large bowl, beat whipping cream, sour cream, powdered sugar, and vanilla with an electric mixer on medium speed until stiff peaks form. Frost top and sides of cake. Garnish cake with pink-and-white curls. Makes 12 servings.

Fudgy Brownie Bites

Shown on *page 110*.

Infuse these brownies with orange liqueur, top them with a chocolate glaze, drizzle with more chocolate, and cut into diamond shapes.

½	cup butter (no substitutes)
2	ounces unsweetened chocolate, cut up
2	eggs
¾	cup sugar
⅓	cup orange marmalade
2	teaspoons Grand Marnier or other orange liqueur
¾	cup all-purpose flour
½	teaspoon baking powder
	Shiny Chocolate Glaze
2	ounces milk chocolate, cut up
1	teaspoon shortening

Preheat oven to 350°F. Line an 8×8×2-inch baking pan with foil. Grease foil; set aside.

In a medium saucepan, melt butter and the unsweetened chocolate over low heat, stirring occasionally. Remove from heat. Cool slightly (about 5 minutes). Stir in eggs, sugar, orange marmalade, and Grand Marnier. Stir in flour and baking powder. Spread batter into the foil-lined pan.

Bake in the preheated oven for 30 minutes or till a wooden toothpick inserted near the center comes out clean. Cool in pan on a wire rack. Using the edges of the foil, lift brownies from the pan. Carefully remove the foil.

Pour Shiny Chocolate Glaze over brownies, spreading evenly. Let stand for 5 minutes. Cut brownies into 24 rectangles with a long, sharp knife.

Before serving, melt the milk chocolate and the shortening in a small, heavy saucepan over low heat, stirring constantly. Place chocolate mixture in a heavy-duty self-sealing plastic bag; snip a small corner from the bag. Drizzle chocolate mixture in a zigzag pattern over each brownie. Let stand about 30 minutes or until chocolate sets. Makes 24 brownies.

Shiny Chocolate Glaze: In a small saucepan, melt 2 ounces bittersweet or semisweet chocolate, cut up, and 2 tablespoons butter over low heat, stirring occasionally. Remove from heat. Stir in ¾ cup sifted powdered sugar, 4 teaspoons hot water, and 1 teaspoon finely shredded orange peel.

Espresso Milk Shake

Shown on *page 110*.

A triple dose of coffee flavor creates an intriguing after-dinner drink.

1	quart coffee-flavor ice cream
⅓	cup chocolate liqueur
2	tablespoons brewed espresso, cooled
2	tablespoons milk
	Snowflake Shards

Place ice cream, liqueur, espresso, and milk in a blender. Cover; blend until smooth. Add more milk, if necessary, for shakelike consistency. If desired, garnish each drink with a Chocolate Snowflake Shard. Serve immediately. Makes 6 servings.

Triple Chocolate Truffles

Shown on *page 111*.

If you think truffles can't get any richer, try melting a small amount of semisweet chocolate or milk chocolate, and drizzling it on top.

12	ounces semisweet chocolate, coarsely chopped
½	of an 8-ounce package cream cheese, softened and cut up
4	teaspoons instant coffee crystals
1⅓	cups milk chocolate or semisweet chocolate pieces
2	tablespoons shortening
2	ounces milk chocolate or semisweet chocolate, coarsely chopped
	Unsweetened cocoa powder

In a medium-size heavy saucepan, cook and stir semisweet chocolate over very low heat. Remove from heat; stir in the cream cheese until combined. Stir together coffee crystals and 1 teaspoon water; add to the chocolate mixture and stir until smooth. Cover and chill about 2 hours or until firm.

Line a baking sheet with waxed paper. Use 2 spoons to shape the truffle mixture into 1-inch balls; place balls on prepared baking sheet. Cover and chill for 1 to 2 hours or until firm.

In a heavy saucepan, cook and stir the milk chocolate pieces and shortening over low heat until melted and smooth. Remove from heat; cool to room temperature.

Use a fork to dip the truffles into the chocolate mixture, allowing excess chocolate to drip back into saucepan. Return truffles to baking sheet; chill about 30 minutes or until firm.

In a small heavy saucepan, cook and stir the 2 ounces chocolate over low heat until melted and smooth. Drizzle over the tops of some of the truffles. Chill for a few minutes or until set. Roll remaining truffles in unsweetened cocoa powder.

To store, place truffles in a tightly covered container in the refrigerator. Let stand at room temperature about 30 minutes before serving. Makes 30 truffles.

Written by **Becky Mollenkamp**   Photographed by **Scott Little**   Project designer **Carrie Naumann**

gourmet gifts

to: Tim

love: Shannon

Satisfy their appetites (and your budget) by making everyone on your holiday list a present that looks as good as it tastes.

CANDY IS DANDY

Turn an inexpensive pencil or empty box into a sweet gift, *opposite*. Cover the box with decorative paper. Hot-glue a ribbon along the bottom and lid, leaving a small loop on the front top edge for a handle. Fill the finished box with bite-size Pistachio and Dried Cherry Nougat in small candy cups.

BOTTLED UP

Thyme and Orange Vinegar, *right*, is a no-fuss gift for coworkers, teachers, and neighbors. Dress it up by wrapping ribbon around the length of the bottle and then around the neck, creating a collar. Make the coordinated tag by gluing leaf shapes, available at scrapbooking and crafts stores, to a colored label; attach with ribbon.

Food is the quickest way to a person's heart. Let loved ones know you really care by baking a gift they will remember.

HAPPY HO-HO-HO HOLIDAYS

The best things come in threes, including our seasoned nuts in adorable "ho-ho-ho" bags. Stuff each of the velvet bags with a plastic baggie filled with nuts. Make a small gift-shape tag and place it in the pocket.

THROW IN THE TOWEL

Easy-to-make Cranberry Muffins look even more special when they arrive in a container crafted with care. Stitch simple snowflake shapes, cut from white felt, onto red felt circles. Trim the circles with pinking shears. Pin the finished circles onto a green tea towel; sew in place.

MATCHED SET

Have fun with gift wrap and make the outside reflect what's inside, *opposite*. This cute wreath wall hanging, attached to the lid, hints at the tin's contents—a tasty Basil Walnut Pesto Wreath bread.

IN A JAM

Make a large batch of Pepper Jelly and give small, jazzy jars of it to all your friends and family, *right*. Print labels (see page 129 for template) onto adhesive-backed paper; cut out. Attach to the front and lid of the jar. Cut a 2-foot length of crepe paper from a roll of streamers. Cut in half lengthwise using pinking shears. Gather paper in small accordion folds. Secure the layers to the lid with double-sided tape. Hot-glue ribbon around the rim.

When it comes to gift giving, style is nearly as important as substance. Take time to make every present look pretty.

SWEET SURPRISE

Fill a square tray with Candy-Cane Twists. Cut two strips of paper about half as wide as the container and long enough to wrap around it. Layer the papers; finish the edges with decorative scissors and a hole punch. Wrap papers around the tray and secure them with tape. Attach a matching label to the top.

CHEESE, PLEASE

For a Christmas twist on the traditional cheese log, give Cilantro-Jalapeño Cheese Spread, single-serving style, with reminders of a favorite holiday tale. Cut a mouse shape out of adhesive-backed felt. Tie a bow and small jingle bell to the tail. Adhere the felt mouse to the cheese-filled ramekin. Stick a smaller mouse on a gift tag; tie the tag to a spreader.

Cranberry Muffins

Shown on *page 119* and *above left.*

1	cup fresh cranberries
2	tablespoons sugar
2	cups all-purpose flour
¼	to ½ cup sugar
4	teaspoons baking powder
1	teaspoon finely shredded orange peel
½	teaspoon salt
1	egg, beaten
¾	cup milk
¼	cup butter, melted

Coarse sugar

Preheat oven to 400°F. Grease twelve to fourteen 2½-inch muffin cups or line with paper bake cups. In a medium bowl, toss cranberries with 2 tablespoons sugar; set aside.

In a large bowl, combine flour, ¼ to ½ cup sugar, baking powder, orange peel, and salt; stir well. In a small bowl, combine egg, milk, and butter. Make a well in center of flour mixture; add egg mixture and cranberries. Stir just until moistened. Spoon into prepared muffin cups. Sprinkle tops with coarse sugar.

Bake in the preheated oven about 15 minutes or until golden. Cool on a wire rack. Makes 12 to 14 muffins.

Basil-Walnut Pesto Wreaths

Shown on *page 120* and *above right.*

Shape each portion of dough into a 6-inch-diameter wreath to fit an 8- to 10-inch gift tin. Separate and turn the slices enough so you can see the cut sides.

⅓	cup chopped walnuts, toasted
3	large cloves garlic, quartered
4	cups loosely packed fresh basil leaves (about 3½ ounces)
⅓	cup olive oil
⅓	cup grated Parmesan cheese
2	tablespoons lemon juice
¼	teaspoon salt
1	16-ounce package hot roll mix
1	egg, slightly beaten
1	tablespoon water

For pesto, place walnuts in a food processor or blender; cover and process or blend until finely chopped. Add garlic; cover and process just until blended. Add basil leaves. With machine running, gradually add oil in a thin, steady stream, processing until the mixture is combined and slightly chunky, stopping to scrape down sides if necessary. Add Parmesan cheese, lemon juice, and salt. Cover and process

or blend just until combined. Set pesto aside.

Prepare hot roll mix according to package directions. After kneading, divide dough into 2 portions; cover and let rest for 5 minutes. Grease 2 baking sheets; set aside.

Turn dough portions out onto a lightly floured surface. Roll each portion to a 14×9-inch rectangle. Spread half of the pesto atop each rectangle to within ½ inch of edges. Starting from a long side of each, roll up into a spiral; seal seams.

Place dough rolls on prepared baking sheets. Attach ends of each roll together to form a circle; pinch seams to seal. Using a sharp knife, cut slits at ¾-inch intervals around each ring. Gently turn each slice so cut edge of each slice shows.

Cover and let rise in a warm place until nearly double (about 30 to 40 minutes).

Preheat oven to 375°F. Combine egg and water; brush onto wreaths. Bake in the preheated oven for 18 to 20 minutes or until golden. Carefully remove wreaths from baking sheets. Cool slightly on wire racks. Makes 2 wreaths (8 servings each).

Shown on *page 123* and *above left.*

Reheating directions: Preheat oven to 350°F. Wrap one wreath in foil; place on a baking sheet. Place in oven for 12 to 15 minutes or until heated through.

Cilantro-Jalapeño Cheese Spread

Shown on *page 123* and *above left.*

1   cup shredded Monterey Jack cheese (4 ounces)
1   cup shredded sharp cheddar cheese (4 ounces)
1   8-ounce package cream cheese, softened
3   tablespoons finely chopped red sweet pepper
3   tablespoons snipped fresh cilantro
1   medium fresh jalapeño chile pepper, seeded and finely chopped*
1   tablespoon milk
½   teaspoon Worcestershire sauce
    Jalapeño pepper slices (optional)

In a large bowl, stir together the Monterey Jack, cheddar, and cream cheeses. Stir in sweet pepper, cilantro, chopped jalapeño pepper, milk, and Worcestershire sauce until combined.

Transfer mixture to two 10-ounce ramekins or bowls. Cover and chill for 2 hours before serving or for up to 3 days. If desired, garnish with jalapeño pepper slices. Makes 2 cups.

*Note: Because hot chile peppers, such as jalapeños, contain volatile oils that can burn your skin and eyes, avoid direct contact with chiles as much as possible. When working with chile peppers, wear plastic or rubber gloves. If your bare hands do touch the chile peppers, wash your hands and nails well with soap and water.

Pepper Jelly

Shown on *page 121* and *above right.*

Be sure to sterilize the canning jars before filling. Wash the jars in hot, soapy water and rinse thoroughly. Then place them in boiling water for 10 minutes.

1½ cups cranberry juice (not low-calorie)
1   cup vinegar
2   to 4 fresh jalapeño chile peppers, halved*
5   cups sugar
½   of a 6-ounce package (1 foil pouch) liquid fruit pectin

In a medium-size enamel, stainless-steel, or nonstick saucepan, combine cranberry juice, vinegar, and jalapeño peppers. Bring to boiling; reduce heat. Simmer, covered, for 10 minutes. Strain mixture through a sieve, pressing with the back of a spoon to remove all the liquid; measure 2 cups. Discard pulp.

In a 6-quart heavy kettle, combine the 2 cups liquid and sugar. Bring to a full rolling boil over high heat, stirring constantly. Quickly stir in pectin. Return to a full rolling boil; boil for 1 minute, stirring constantly. Remove from heat. Quickly skim off foam with a metal spoon.

Ladle at once into hot, sterilized half-pint canning jars, leaving a ¼-inch headspace. Wipe jar rims; adjust lids. Process in a boiling-water canner for 5 minutes (start timing when water returns to boil). Remove jars and cool on a wire rack for 2 to 3 days or until set. Makes 5 half-pints.

Candy-Cane Twists

Shown on *page 122* and *top left.*

Kids old enough to roll a ball of dough into a rope can help shape these sparkling canes. Color part of the dough red if you like.

1   cup butter, softened
1   cup sifted powdered sugar
1   egg
½   teaspoon vanilla
Dash salt
2½   cups all-purpose flour
¼   cup finely crushed peppermint
        candies
Few drops red food coloring
        (optional)
Coarse or colored sugar
Finely crushed peppermint candies
        (optional)

In a large mixing bowl, beat butter with an electric mixer on medium to high speed for 30 seconds. Add powdered sugar; beat until combined. Beat in egg, vanilla, and salt. Beat in as much of the flour as you can with the mixer. Stir in any remaining flour with a wooden spoon. Divide dough in half. Knead ¼ cup crushed peppermint candies into one half of the dough. If desired, knead red food coloring into the peppermint dough to slightly tint; leave remaining half of dough plain. Cover and chill doughs about 30 minutes until easy to handle.

Preheat oven to 375°F. Work with half of each dough at a time, keeping remaining dough chilled until ready to use. For each cookie, on a lightly floured surface, shape a 1-inch ball of plain dough into a 4- or 5-inch rope. Repeat with a 1-inch ball of peppermint dough. Place ropes side by side and twist together. Pinch ends to seal. Form twisted ropes into a cane. Place canes 2 inches apart on an ungreased cookie sheet. Sprinkle with sugar and additional crushed candies if desired.

Bake in the preheated oven for 8 to 10 minutes or until edges of cookies are set. Immediately transfer cookies to wire racks and let cool. Makes 32 canes.

To Store: Place cookies in layers separated by waxed paper in an airtight container; cover. Store at room temperature for up to 3 days or freeze for up to 1 month.

Thyme-and-Orange Vinegar

Shown on *page 117* and *middle left.*

This recipe makes a delicious low-fat salad dressing.

8   cups white wine vinegar
1   750-milliliter bottle dry white
        wine (3¼ cups)
½   cup packed fresh thyme sprigs
1   medium orange
Fresh thyme sprigs, rinsed and dried
        (optional)

In a large stainless-steel, enameled, or nonstick kettle, combine vinegar, wine, and the ½ cup thyme. Using a vegetable peeler, remove the orange portion of the peel from the orange in narrow strips; add the strips to the saucepan. (Juice orange; reserve juice for another use.) Bring the vinegar mixture almost to boiling. Remove from heat. Cover loosely with 100-percent-cotton cheesecloth; let stand about 3 hours or until cooled to room temperature.

Pour into three 1-quart jars. Cover with nonmetallic lids (or cover with plastic wrap and tightly seal with metal lids). Let stand in a cool, dark place for 2 weeks.

Line a colander with several layers of 100-percent-cotton cheesecloth or coffee filters. Place colander over a large bowl. Pour vinegar mixture through the colander into the bowl. Discard solids.

Transfer strained vinegar to 1-pint jars or bottles. If desired, add a sprig of thyme to each jar or bottle. Cover jars or bottles with nonmetallic lids (or cover with plastic wrap and tightly seal with metal lids). Store vinegar in a cool, dark place for up to 6 months. Makes 5 (½-pint) gifts.

Pistachio and Dried Cherry Nougat

Shown on *page 116* and *opposite bottom*.

Butter
Cornstarch
1½ cups sugar
1 tablespoon cornstarch
1 cup light-color corn syrup
2 egg whites
1 teaspoon vanilla
1½ teaspoons finely shredded lemon peel
¾ cup chopped pistachio nuts
¾ cup dried tart red cherries

Line a 9×9×2-inch pan with foil, extending foil over edges of pan. Butter foil; sprinkle with a small amount of cornstarch. Set pan aside.

In a heavy 2-quart saucepan, combine sugar and 1 tablespoon cornstarch. Add corn syrup and ½ cup *water;* mix well. Cook over medium-high heat to boiling, stirring constantly with a wooden spoon to dissolve sugar. (This should take 5 to 7 minutes.) Avoid splashing mixture on sides of pan. Carefully clip a candy thermometer to side of pan.

Cook over medium heat, stirring occasionally until thermometer registers 286°F, soft-crack stage. (This should take 20 to 25 minutes.) Mixture should boil at a moderate and steady rate over entire surface.

Remove saucepan from heat; remove candy thermometer from saucepan. In a large mixing bowl, immediately beat egg whites with a sturdy, freestanding electric mixer on medium speed until stiff peaks form (tips stand straight).

Gradually pour hot mixture in a thin stream (slightly less than ⅛-inch diameter) into egg whites, beating with the electric mixer on high speed and scraping sides of bowl occasionally (about 3 minutes).

Add vanilla. Continue beating on high speed, scraping sides of bowl occasionally until candy becomes very thick and less glossy. When beaters are lifted, mixture should fall in a ribbon, but mound on itself, then slowly disappear into the remaining mixture (5 to 6 minutes).

Immediately stir in lemon peel, pistachio nuts, and dried cherries. Quickly turn candy mixture into prepared pan. While candy is warm, score into 1×1-inch pieces. When candy is firm, use foil to lift it out of pan; cut candy into pieces. Wrap each piece in clear plastic wrap. Makes 81 pieces.

To store: Keep wrapped candies in an airtight container at room temperature for up to two weeks.

Herbed Toasted Almonds

Shown on *page 118*.

Make one batch of these well-seasoned nuts for giving and another to keep on hand for a holiday snack.

½ pound whole almonds (2 cups)
1 tablespoon cooking oil
1 teaspoon dried basil, crushed
¾ teaspoon dried thyme, crushed
¼ teaspoon garlic salt

Preheat oven to 350°F. Place almonds in a single layer in a shallow baking pan. Drizzle with oil and sprinkle with basil, thyme, and garlic salt. Stir to coat.

Bake in the preheated oven for 10 to 15 minutes or until nuts are toasted, stirring every 5 minutes. Drain on paper towels. Cool to room temperature. Store in a sealed plastic bag or container. Makes 2 cups.

Make-ahead tip: Store almonds in a tightly closed container in the refrigerator for up to 1 week or in the freezer for up to 1 month.

Spicy-Sweet Nut Mix

Shown on *page 118*.

With an intriguing blend of sweetness and heat, these nuts are a treat that's hard to stop eating.

¾ cup lightly salted cashews
⅛ teaspoon cayenne pepper
2 teaspoons soy sauce
2 teaspoons honey
2 tablespoons pure maple syrup
1 teaspoon butter, melted
1 cup pecan halves

Preheat oven to 350°F. For the spicy cashews, line a 15×10×1-inch baking pan with foil. Grease foil; set aside. In a food processor or blender, place ¼ *cup* of the cashews. Cover and process or blend until finely ground. Stir together ground cashews and cayenne pepper. In a medium bowl, combine soy sauce and honey. Add remaining whole cashews; stir to coat. Add ground cashew mixture; stir well. Spread mixture in prepared pan. Bake in the preheated oven for 10 to 15 minutes or until browned, stirring two or three times. Cool completely. Break into pieces.

For maple-candied pecans, line a 15×10×1-inch baking pan with foil. Grease foil; set aside. In a medium bowl, combine maple syrup and melted butter. Add pecans; toss to coat. Spread pecans in the prepared pan. Bake in the preheated 350°F oven for 10 to 15 minutes, stirring twice. Cool completely.

To serve, combine both types of nuts in a bowl. Store in a sealed plastic bag or airtight container. Makes 2 cups.

Chili Nuts Santa Fe

Shown on *pages 118* and *right*.

The egg white helps the spice mixture cling to the nuts so the zesty flavor is evenly distributed.

1   egg white
1   tablespoon frozen orange juice
      concentrate, thawed
¼   cup sugar
1   tablespoon chili powder
1   teaspoon garlic powder
½   teaspoon ground cumin
¼   teaspoon ground black
      pepper
¼   to ½ teaspoon cayenne
      pepper
¼   teaspoon celery salt
¼   teaspoon ground cinnamon
3   cups peanuts or mixed nuts
Nonstick cooking spray

Preheat oven to 325°F. In a large bowl, combine egg white, juice concentrate, sugar, chili powder, garlic powder, cumin, black pepper, cayenne pepper, celery salt, and cinnamon. Stir in nuts; toss to coat.

Line a 15×10×1-inch pan with foil; spray with nonstick cooking spray. Spread nuts on foil. Bake in the preheated oven for 20 minutes, stirring twice. Cool; break apart large clusters. Store in an airtight container at room temperature for up to 1 week. Makes 3 cups.

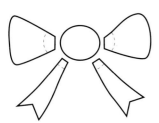

Ho-Ho-Ho Bag
Bow pattern

Ho-Ho-Ho Bag

Shown on *pages 118–119* and *above*.

MATERIALS

⅓ yard of red velveteen
1×9½-inch strip of white fake fur
Sewing thread: white and red
⅜ yard of wired cream chenille ribbon
½ yard of ⅜-inch-wide green
    velvet ribbon
Two silver bells
1 sheet of green-and-white polka-dot
    paper
Glue
Card stock: 1 sheet each of white
    and green
Fine-tip black marking pen

INSTRUCTIONS

Cut a 9½-inch square for the bag and a 3½-inch square for the bag pocket from red velveteen.

Fold the top edge of the bag under ½ inch; then fold under again 1½ inches to form the cuff. Use a ¼-inch seam allowance to sew the cuff in place.

Topstitch the white fake fur strip to the top edge of the cuff using white sewing thread.

Fold three edges of the 3½-inch red velveteen square under ¼ inch; press. Fold the top edge under ½ inch; press and topstitch ⅛ inch inside the folded edge with red thread. Cut a 3½-inch length from the wired cream chenille ribbon; topstitch it ½ inch below the top pocket edge.

Cut lettering pieces from the wired cream chenille ribbon as follows: two 1¼-inch pieces and one ¾-inch piece for the letter "H," and one 4¼-inch piece for the letter "O." Topstitch the pieces to the front center of the pocket.

Fold the 9½-inch red velveteen square in half. Position the pocket on one-half of the bag; unfold the bag and topstitch the pocket along the side and bottom edges.

Cut an 8-inch and a 10-inch length from green velvet ribbon. Fold the bag in half with right sides facing, sandwiching the ribbon lengths along the cuff between the fabric layers and aligning the ribbon ends with the fabric raw edges; sew the sides and bottom of the bag. Turn the bag right side out.

Thread a silver bell onto each ribbon length; knot the ribbon ends.

To make the card, cut a 3½-inch square from green-and-white polka-dot paper and fold it in half. Cut a bow (pattern at *left*) and a ¼×3½-inch strip from white card stock. Glue the strip vertically to the front center of the card. Glue the bow to the top of the strip.

To make the label, cut a 1⅛×½-inch strip from white card stock and mat it with green card stock. Write a message on the label with a fine-tip black marking pen. Glue the label to the front of the card.

Holly Wreath Tin

Shown on *page 120* and *right.*

MATERIALS

Card stock: 4 sheets of light green and 3 sheets each of medium green and dark green
Double-stick tape
1 sheet of shiny red sticker-back puff paper
Circle punches: small and large
8-inch-round white tin with lid

INSTRUCTIONS

To make the wreath base, cut a 7-inch-diameter circle from light green card stock. Cut a 3-inch-diameter circle in the center of the 7-inch-diameter circle.

Use the holly leaf pattern, *right,* to cut 20 to 30 leaves from each color of green card stock. Fold the leaves in half lengthwise; unfold. Write the recipient's name or a message on one leaf. Use double-stick tape to adhere the leaves in an overlapping pattern onto the wreath base, following the photo, *above right.* Punch small circles from red sticker-back puff paper, peel off the paper backings, and press the circles onto random leaves.

Punch small and large circles from red sticker-back puff paper and apply the circles to the outside of the tin. Use double-stick tape to adhere the wreath to the tin lid.

Holly Leaf Tin
Holly leaf patterns

Pepper Jelly Label

festive tables

Infuse holiday spirit into your
Christmas gatherings using these
festive table-setting ideas.

serving up

Style

Discover new ways to decorate your holiday table.
Set a festive scene with these fresh presentations.

Before the food and frivolity, behold the table—a blank canvas of decorating opportunity. This party season, set the mood for a family feast or an intimate gathering with friends by making your dining table a worthy focal point. Tables, after all, are one of the easiest changes for ho-hum holiday decor. Looking for some creative inspiration? Our four presentations serve up delicious style: Set a red-and-gold showstopper that has a fresh new attitude; go casual with twigs and berries; sugar-coat a kid-friendly setting; or, for those who want formality, bedazzle guests with rich jewel-tone layers. As wise hosts and hostesses know, it doesn't cost a fortune or take the skills of a designer to make a table look fabulous.

Written by **Jody Garlock**
Photographed by **Kim Cornelison**
Produced by **Jill Budden**

tradition with a *twist*

Red and gold veers any holiday soirée to the traditional side. Throw in a heady dose of white and some creative twists, and you have a refreshing and updated take on tradition.

DREAM WEAVER. This festive setting, *opposite,* starts with a wallpaper tablecloth. Cut two strips of embossed wallpaper (the paintable, scrubbable kind that is readily available at home centers) to the table's length. There's no need to adjust the paper's width; just overlap the pieces as needed to fit the table. Use a crafts knife to cut equally spaced slits along each edge of the wallpaper strips and weave red velvet ribbon through the slits.

HAVE A BALL. Elevated on glass candlesticks and sprinkled with glitter, a grouping of inexpensive glass-ball ornaments creates a striking centerpiece. Use glue to write a letter on each ornament, *below left,* sprinkle with glitter, and then shake off excess glitter. Place each ornament on a candlestick. The ornament will

rest in the hole designed for a taper, but for extra security, add a piece of double-stick tape to the bottom of the ornament.

BEARING GIFTS. Earn the title "Super Hostess" by leaving a surprise on each guest's chair, *below middle.* Instead of ribbon, wind thin gold wire around the gift, randomly looping red eyelets through the wire for a fun embellishment. The name tag—a die-cut ornament-shape designed for scrapbooking—doubles as a place marker. Use a computer to print a greeting and name on vellum, and then glue it to the die-cut shape. A sheer seat cover adds a wisp of elegance to the chair. Cut fabric so it hangs over the seat about two inches on the front and sides. Use fusible web to hem along the edges. Hand-stitch ribbon ties to the back.

MIX IT UP. Though not a matched set, a red-and-gold color scheme unites the china, *below right.* The lesson learned: Mixing things up is perfectly fine in more traditional settings.

Presentation counts—and it starts with the table. Let yours set the mood for a dinner to remember.

casual *affair*

Take a cue from the trends in home decor and go casual with your holiday table. With earthy colors and nature-inspired embellishments, this table maintains an easygoing attitude with square and rectangular plates and decorations.

DASHING DETAILS. Let fabrics launch the look and set the mood of your table, *opposite.* The place mats' rough-and-tumble burlaplike fabric is gussied up with a velvety design and was a license to mix rugged with refined. If you're pinching pennies (and who isn't at the holidays?), shop the remnant piles at fabrics stores.

CENTER OF ATTENTION. You can enjoy this showstopping centerpiece, *opposite,* all season. Group pillar candles (we used nine) in the center of the table. Add fake snow to visually soften the area around the candles. Create a wreath base by removing the stems from fake

berries with twiggy branches, available at crafts stores, and loosely braiding the twigs around the candles. Place a layer of red berries (we used fresh hypericum) in the wreath, framing the candles. Wrap a wide ribbon around the candle grouping and secure with a straight pin.

NO-SEW SOLUTION. Easy-make linens, *opposite* and *above left,* drape the table to soften hard edges without the formality of a tablecloth. Cut decorator fabric into 18-inch squares. Use double-stick fusible web to hem two opposite edges of each place mat, and then use it to embellish the remaining two edges with 1½-inch-wide ribbon. The table runner is a 4-inch-wide white satin ribbon.

COVERING YOUR BACK. Dangling chair-back wreaths, *above right,* answer the call for casual holiday cheer. The 3-inch wreaths are a scaled-down version of the centerpiece. Mold real or fake berry twigs into the desired shape, or wrap them around a miniature grapevine wreath. Wrap a ribbon around the top of the chair several times, securing one loose end with tape, and tie the wreath to the remaining loose end.

elegant *dining*

Rich jewel tones, sumptuous fabrics, and lush layers lend an air of sophistication to this setting, ideal for an intimate dinner. The table is layered in plum and burgundy silks and velvets; the monotone color scheme adds to the beauty.

SERENE SCENE. Create the layered look by cutting and hemming a piece of burgundy velvet fabric to fit the whole table, *opposite.* Drape three plum silk table runners across the width of the table; they double as place mats. Add a fourth runner the length of the table to define the centerpiece. The topiaries are 18-inch-tall florist's-foam cones covered with batting and dressed with silk plum slipcovers. Sheer ribbon and beaded snowflakes dress up the outer two trees, while burgundy beads wrap the center one.

ORNAMENTAL FLAVOR. Snowflake ornament party favors, *above left,* are easily made by stringing beads on wire. Get maximum mileage out of the handmade ornaments by using the wire loop to hang them from wineglasses.

PLATE PANACHE. The snowflake decal that appears to be etched into the salad plate, *above right,* adds an illusion of grandeur. It's actually just a piece of vellum inserted between the two plates. Cut a piece of clear vellum the same size as the bottom of the top plate. Center a die-cut snowflake-shape, available in crafts stores, on the vellum circle. Hold the die cut in place, and apply gold stencil cream on the uncovered part of the vellum. Remove the die cut, revealing a translucent snowflake.

kidding
around

Forget the crystal, the china, and the fine linens. In other words, forget the stress. With a paper tablecloth, melamine plates, and plastic tumblers, this footloose-and-fancy-free table is perfectly suited for the young—and the young at heart.

JUST FOR FUN. Throwaway style doesn't have to lack pizzazz. This tablecloth, *opposite,* gets the presentation off to a sugary-sweet start. Purchase paper on a roll from an art-supply store, or start with a paper tablecloth. Place a bowl (ours was 4½ inches in diameter) on the bottom edge of the paper, and trace around it about halfway. Draw a line the length of the paper as a guide for where to end each scallop. Cut out the scallops with scissors. Use a pushpin or hot glue to attach a gumdrop in the center of each scallop.

SWEET TREAT. This table decoration, *below left,* will leave kids with visions of lollipops dancing in their heads. Wrap a sturdy box with tissue paper; adhere it with clear tape. Cut a band of contrasting-color tissue paper with scallop edges; tape it to the top of the box. Fill the box with gumdrops, and then insert lollipops into the candies.

PLAY TIME. This napkin-cum-artist's-pouch, *below right,* lets kids while away a meal by decorating the tree-shape place mat. Unfold a paper napkin. Fold the bottom edge up toward the front of the napkin, about one-third of the way. Fold the sides toward the back of the napkin, about one-third of the way on each side, forming a pocket on the front. Add names with letter stickers. For the place mats, cut Christmas-tree shapes from drawing paper. ❋

For more tabletop ideas: www.bhg.com/sipcenterpieces

blue
christmas

Draw inspiration from the **FRIGID WEATHER** outside and host a MONOGRAM holiday party in **ICY SHADES** of blue.

Written by **SHELLEY STEWART**   Projects designed by **WENDY MUSGRAVE**   Photographed by **KIM CORNELISON**

Instructions begin on page 146.

BLUE SOCKS

A stocking satin-stitched with your guest's initial, *opposite*, makes an unexpected spot to tuck in silverware at each place setting—and it's a fun take-home favor.

TABLE FEAST

Enter into an icy wonderland with a holiday scheme in cool, contemporary tones. Monograms on chair swags, place settings, and an elegant table runner play on the letter theme of the holiday gathering.

UNDER WRAPS Strips of icy blue fabric sewn together make an elegant striped sleeve for a wine bottle, *left*. Present the gift in style by cinching the bottle neck with a lemon-yellow bow and draping a beaded-letter ornament—customized for the recipient—over the sleeve.

ON THE RUN Create a dramatic centerpiece by embellishing a silk runner with a variety of different sizes and styles of rubber stamp letters along its border, *opposite, top left*.

ON EDGE Enliven the corner of a plain linen napkin with a stamped initial and a sprinkling of blue beads attached with thread, *opposite, top right*. Keep the napkin neat and tidy until it's needed with a sheer blue bow.

CHARMED Simple to wrap around the stem of a wineglass to help party guests keep tabs on their drink as they mingle, these wineglass charms are made from crafts wire threaded with shimmering silver-blue beads, *opposite, bottom left*. Each coiled strand is completed with a metal letter charm.

RECIPE POUCH A stamped silk pouch filled with recipe cards makes a great party favor, *opposite, bottom right*. When the food is as scrumptious as the decor is beautiful, your guests will love receiving recipe cards that have the evening's complete menu printed on them.

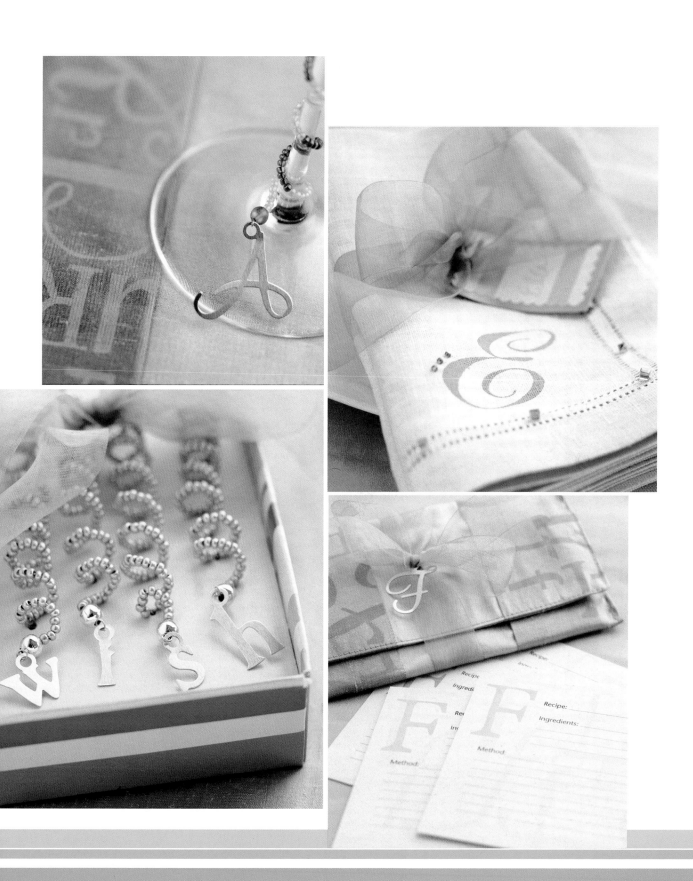

ALL-PURPOSE LETTER STAMP

MATERIALS

Computer and printer
Crafts foam
1½×1¾-inch piece of
1-inch-thick pine board
Crafts glue

INSTRUCTIONS

To make a letter stamp, use your computer and printer to print letters in a variety of fonts and sizes up to 2¼ inches tall. Transfer the letters onto crafts foam and carefully cut out. Apply a thick coat of crafts glue to one side of the pine. Arrange a letter front side down onto the wet glue. Let dry.

TABLE RUNNER

Shown *opposite, top right* and on page 143.

MATERIALS

Two colors of silk fabric
Colored stamp pad
Needle and sewing thread
Matching broadcloth
Computer and printer
Two 6-inch-squares of
paper-backed fusible web

INSTRUCTIONS

Determine the desired finished length of your table runner; subtract 4 inches. Use this measurement to cut an 11½-inch-wide center section from one silk fabric and two 3½-inch-wide side border strips from the second silk fabric. Also cut two 3½×16½-inch end border strips from the second fabric.

Make letter stamps following the All-Purpose Letter Stamp directions above.

Test the stamp and ink on a scrap first, and then stamp the letter images on the side and end border strips. Repeat the stamp as many times as necessary to completely cover each strip. Let the ink dry.

With right sides together, sew a side border strip to each long edge of the center section with a ½-inch seam allowance. Press the seam allowances away from the center section. Sew an end border strip to each short edge. Press the seam allowances toward the border strips.

Use the pieced front as a pattern to cut a matching shape from the broadcloth for the back. With right sides together, sew the front to the back with a ½-inch seam allowance, leaving a 3-inch opening on one side. Trim the seams and corners. Turn the table runner right side out and press. Slip-stitch the opening closed.

For the monogram, use your computer and printer to print a 4-inch-tall letter; cut out the letter. Fuse a square of web to the back of a 6-inch-square of silk, following the manufacturer's instructions. Place the letter right side down on the paper backing. Trace around the letter and cut out. Remove the paper backing. Position the letter, web side down, centered on one end of the table runner about 1 inch from the end border; fuse. Repeat for the opposite end.

CHAIR SWAG

Shown *opposite, middle right* and on page 143.

MATERIALS

Two colors of silk fabric
Needle and sewing thread
Paper-backed ½-inch-wide
fusible-web tape
2¾-inch beaded tassel
Sew-in craft-weight interfacing
Iron-on crystal letter
Hook-and-loop sticky dots

INSTRUCTIONS

Measure the distance around the slats on the chair back; add 6 inches. Use this measurement to cut two 3½-inch-wide strips from one of the silk fabrics for the center section and two 1¾-inch-wide strips from the second for the borders.

Center one 3½-inch-wide center-section strip on the other with wrong sides together. Press under ¼ inch on one long edge of the 1¾-inch-wide border strip. With right sides facing, use a ¼-inch seam allowance to sew the opposite edge of the border strip to one long edge of the layered center section. Press all seam allowances away from the center section. Apply fusible-web tape over the pressed edge of the strip, following the manufacturer's instructions. Remove the paper backing. Fold the pressed edge to the back of the center section, covering the machine stitching; fuse. Repeat on the opposite edge.

Press under ¼ inch twice on one short edge of the chair wrap; slip-stitch in place. To shape the point, press under ¼ inch on the remaining short edge and bring the corners up to meet on the back, creating a V shape; press. Position the tassel at the point, tucking the hanging loop between the fabric layers. Slip-stitch the edges together and to the back of the wrap, securing the tassel in the stitching.

Apply the crystal letter to the front of the wrap 2 inches above the point. Position the wrap around the chair back and apply hook-and-loop sticky dots to secure.

SILVERWARE STOCKING

Shown *bottom right* and on *page 142*.

MATERIALS

Tracing paper
Two colors of silk fabric
Embroidery floss
Needle and sewing thread
Sew-in craft-weight interfacing
Wired pom-pom trim

INSTRUCTIONS

Trace the stocking and cuff patterns on *page 149* onto tracing paper; cut out. Use a ½-inch seam allowance with right sides facing when sewing the pieces together.

Use contrasting two-ply embroidery floss to satin-stitch a ⅞-inch-tall monogram onto one piece of silk fabric. For the cuff front, trim the monogrammed silk into a 6×5-inch rectangle, centering the letter 1⅛ inches above a 6-inch edge. For the cuff back, cut a second 6×5-inch rectangle from the same color of silk fabric.

From the second silk fabric, cut two 6×8-inch rectangles for the stocking front and back. From the interfacing, cut two 6×8-inch rectangles and two 6×5-inch rectangles. Pin the interfacing rectangles to the wrong side of the corresponding silk rectangles. Sew the bottom edge of the cuff front to a 6-inch edge of the stocking front. Sew the remaining rectangles together in the same manner for the back. Press the seam allowances open.

With the interfacing side up, position the stocking pattern on the front rectangles, aligning the cuff line on the pattern with the seam line and centering the monogram on the cuff. Trace around the pattern onto the interfacing. For the facing, draw a 2-inch line upward from each top corner of the traced stocking shape; connect the ends. Cut out

the silk/interfacing stocking shape ½ inch beyond the traced lines. Cut the interfacing only along the top traced line of the cuff. For the stocking back, flip the pattern over and repeat on the pieced back rectangles. To hem the facing, press under ¼ inch on the top edges of the stocking front and back; sew ⅛ inch from each pressed edge. Sew the stocking front to the back, leaving the hemmed facing edges open. Trim the seams, and clip the curves. Turn the stocking right side out. Finger-press the seams. Turn the facing down into the stocking and press. Tack facing in place at the side seams.

Wrap pom-pom trim around the bottom edge of the cuff and sew in place.

NAPKINS

Shown on *page 145*.

MATERIALS

Napkins
Stencil
Spray adhesive
Water-based fabric ink
Stencil brush
Assorted beads
Matching sewing thread

INSTRUCTIONS

Launder the napkins to remove any sizing; press. Lightly spray the back of the stencil with adhesive and position it on one corner of the napkin. Dip the stencil brush in ink; wipe off almost all the ink with a paper towel. Apply ink to the open areas of the stencil, dabbing the brush onto the napkin with an up-and-down motion. Remove the stencil and let the ink dry. Heat-set the ink, following the manufacturer's instructions. Sew beads onto the napkins, referring to the photograph on *page 145* for placement ideas.

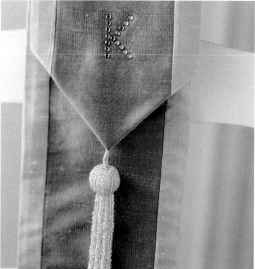

WINE BAG ORNAMENT

Shown *top right* and on *page 144*.

MATERIALS

Wire
Needle-nose pliers
Assorted beads
Wire cutters
Fine cording

INSTRUCTIONS

Wrap one end of the wire around the tip of the needle-nose pliers. Thread beads onto the straight end of the wire in the desired pattern; shape the wire into the letter shape. Twist the wire next to the last bead to secure; trim the excess wire. Tie the letter around the outside of the silk bag with fine cording.

WINEGLASS CHARMS

Shown *above* and on *page 145*.

MATERIALS

18-inch length of wire
Letter charm
Two large beads
Seed beads
Needle-nose pliers
Wire cutters
Wooden dowel or marker

INSTRUCTIONS

Attach a letter to one end of the wire. Thread a large bead onto the wire. Thread seed beads onto the wire in the desired pattern until the beaded area measures about 13½ inches.

Thread the remaining large bead onto the wire. Twist the wire around the tip of the needle-nose pliers to secure the beads, leaving about ½ inch of empty wire between the last bead and the twist. Cut off the excess wire. Wrap the beaded wire around a dowel or marker to spiral; slip off the dowel.

RECIPE ENVELOPE

Shown *above* and on *page 145*.

MATERIALS

Two colors of silk fabric
Colored stamp pad
Needle and sewing thread
1 yard of 1-inch-wide ribbon
Letter charm
Card stock

INSTRUCTIONS

Create letter stamps following the All-Purpose Letter Stamp directions on page 146.

Cut two 3×1½-inch side strips from one of the silk fabrics. Stamp the letters onto one side of the silk strips, repeating as many times as necessary to completely cover each strip. Let the ink dry.

Cut one 4×11½-inch center strip from the remaining silk fabric. With right sides together, sew a side strip to each long edge of the center strip with ½-inch seam allowances. Press the seam allowances away from the center.

Use the pieced front as a pattern to cut a matching shape from the first color of silk for the lining. With right sides together, sew the front to the lining with a ½-inch seam allowance, leaving a 2-inch-wide opening on one side. Trim the seams and corners. Turn the envelope right side out and press. Slip-stitch the opening closed.

To make the pocket, fold up the bottom 3 inches; press and pin. Sew close to the left, top, and right edges of the envelope. To finish, thread the letter charm onto the ribbon, and tie the ribbon into a bow.

Create the recipe cards by cutting card stock into 4×6-inch rectangles. Use a 1½-inch-tall letter stamp (instructions on page 146) to add a monogram to the corner of each card. Handwrite recipes or run the cards through your printer. If desired, you can create additional letter stamps and stamp them onto the card stock with white ink before you add the final monogram.

SILK WINE BAG

Shown *opposite, top right* and on *page 144.*

MATERIALS

Two colors of silk fabric
Needle and matching
    sewing thread
1 yard of 1-inch-wide ribbon
Sew-in medium-
    weight interfacing

INSTRUCTIONS

Measure the distance around a wine bottle; add 2 inches. Measure the wine bottle height and add 3 inches. Use these measurements to cut a rectangle from the interfacing. Cut a large rectangle the same width as the interfacing from each silk fabric.

Cut the silk rectangles into strips of varying widths.

Place one strip right side up on the interfacing, aligning the bottom and side edges. With right sides together, place a contrasting strip on the first strip, aligning the edges. Use a ¼-inch seam allowance to sew the long edges together, sewing through both fabric layers and the interfacing. Open up the top strip and press. Continue adding alternating colored strips to completely cover the interfacing rectangle. Fold the pieced rectangle in half with right sides facing, aligning the seams. Use a ½-inch seam allowance to sew the long edges together for the center back, forming a tube. Do not turn.

Measure the diameter of the circle at the bottom of the fabric tube. Use this measurement to cut a circle of silk and interfacing, adding ½-inch seam allowances. Center the silk circle right side up on the interfacing circle; baste together. Sew the layered circles to the bottom of the tube. Clip the curves and turn the bag right side out.

To hem the top edge, turn under ½ inch twice and slip-stitch in place. Place the wine bottle into the bag, and tie ribbon around the neck.

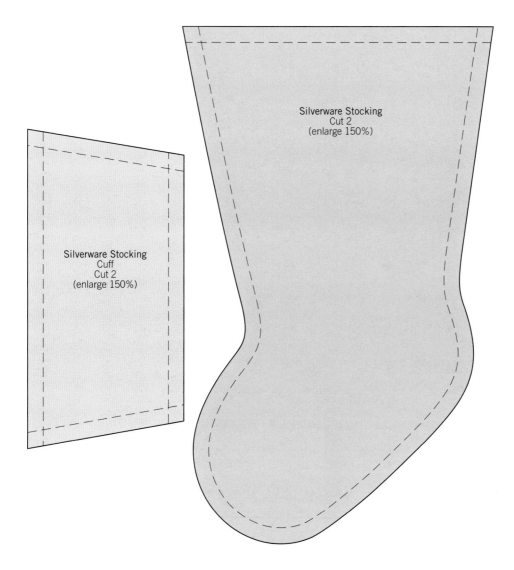

Silverware Stocking
Cut 2
(enlarge 150%)

Silverware Stocking
Cuff
Cut 2
(enlarge 150%)

Seasonal settings

3

Whether you favor a classic Christmas look or a break from tradition, you'll find a scheme to charm your table in these handmade dressings.

DESIGNED BY **CATHY KRAMER**   WRITTEN BY **KRISTIN SCHMITT**
PHOTOGRAPHED BY **GREG SCHEIDEMANN**

traditional
tidings

Holly sprigs and cranberry chains tell a classic tale of Christmas charm on this red-and-green holiday table. Place settings framed by casual felt mats mark a homey spot for each guest. Build a pretty centerpiece with nature's seasonal favorites, and then add simple finishing touches to party-favor bags and napkin rings to complete the setting.

gift bags and place mats Fashion these homespun place mats and gift bags from layers of wool felt, *opposite*. Cut holly leaves in the place mat's red layer and add felt button circles to mimic berries before stitching the rectangular piece to a green base. Cinch scallop-trimmed squares of red and green felt with a length of ribbon adorned with pinecones and berries to capture the gift bag's goodies.

dinnerware Select a controlled mix of dinnerware—green bubble-glass tumblers and softly scalloped white ceramic plates layered over woven wood chargers—to complement your handiwork, *left*.

napkin ring A simple loop of green grosgrain ribbon decorated with a holly sprig hugs silverware and a Christmas-red napkin, *above right*.

centerpiece Cranberries floating above holly leaves and berries in a water-filled glass bowl encircle the centerpiece candle like a wreath, *below*. Add evergreen branches and a cranberry garland to finish the yuletide table decoration.

flashback
fun

Although they're not quite the hues that flavor traditional fare, lime green and aquamarine set a cheerful holiday table reflective of yesteryear's simple style. Mix basic tableware with playful paperwork in the form of table-topping decorations, sprinkle in retro-inspired feather trees and colored tinsel, and let the peppy palette provide the festive splash.

napkin tie A small ornament and a simple tie of tinsel brighten the tableware, *opposite*.

table runner Trim a paper runner to fit just the tabletop, enlivening the length with scalloped and flower-punched edges, *left*. Charlie Brown-style feather trees make modest centerpieces, especially spruced up with a few petite ornament balls and homemade paper tags.

ornament shapes Choose paper in hues and patterns that complement the table's retro scheme. Mounted on card stock and trimmed into photo-framing ornament shapes, paper makes whimsical plate-side decorations, *above left*.

place cards Identify a seat for every guest with ornament place cards fashioned from scrapbooking or wrapping paper and dangled from a length of tinsel ribbon tied around the chair back, *above right*.

stockings Add sparkling buttons and colored tinsel designs to store-bought stockings of green and crème moiré, *below*. Snazzy packages wrapped with fancy paperwork peek out of the stocking tops.

peppermint
punch

The crisp, cool spirit of two-tone candy-cane stripes serve up an energizing scene on this buffet. A striped runner and red-and-white ribbons add tactile embellishments, while candles playing to the theme and various forms of the sweet treat itself keep the serving spread minty fresh.

ribbon candles Trim white pillars with ribbons of various designs and textures for candylike tabletop creations, *opposite left*.

table runner To help make this lively scheme pop, limit tableware to white, clear glass, or shining silver. Set the stage with a white fleece runner trimmed with curvy red stripes and a beaded edge. Intertwine pillar candles of various designs and sizes to dress up the buffet fare, *left*.

martini glasses Sweeten the rim of martini glasses by dipping them in crushed candy canes, *above left*. Add stir sticks adorned with candy-cane shapes.

napkin box Trim a red-paper-wrapped box with layers of red-and-white ribbon for a place to tuck in napkins ringed with peppermint loops, *above right*.

candy-cane candles Straightforward red pillars play into the peppermint scene when decorated with polka-dot ribbon or candy-cane sticks, *below*. Heavy-duty double-stick tape adheres the embellishments to the candles.

INSTRUCTIONS BEGIN ON PAGE 158.

Felt Place Mat

Shown *below,* and on *page 152.*

MATERIALS

- ½ yard each of red and green felt
- Embroidery thread to match red felt
- Sewing thread to match red felt
- Embroidery needle

INSTRUCTIONS

Cut a red felt rectangle the size of a standard place mat. Cut a green felt rectangle 1 inch larger on all sides.

Enlarge the holly leaf pattern on *page 129* using a photocopier; cut out the pattern. Pin the pattern to a corner of the red felt rectangle; cut out the openings. Cut ½-inch-diameter circles from red felt, and tack them in place with red embroidery thread, leaving short tails on the front side of each tack to tie a decorative knot. Use embroidery thread to sew a running stitch down the center of each holly leaf for veins. Lay the red rectangle on top of the green rectangle, centering it on all sides, and top-stitch the felt pieces together.

Paper Photo Ornaments

Shown *below,* and on *page 154.*

MATERIALS

- Patterned, colored, and white card stock
- Photos
- Crafts wire
- Glitter
- Crafts glue

INSTRUCTIONS

For the tag front, cut a circle from patterned card stock in the size you want. For the tag back, cut a second circle from colored card stock. Cut out a shape with angled sides for an ornament top. Cut a 4-inch length of crafts wire and form it into a spiral shape.

Glue the wire spiral to the back of the ornament top shape. Glue the ornament top to the back of the patterned card-stock circle. Glue the colored card-stock circle to the upper back of the patterned card-stock circle.

(1) Cut a photo into a circle smaller than the card-stock circle. Glue it in place on the front of the card-stock circle. Apply glue to the ornament top and the photo edges.

(2) Sprinkle the glue with glitter, tap off the excess, and let dry. Optional: Using a computer, print out a holiday greeting or name. With the text centered, cut out a banner shape. Cut a slit on each side of the photo large enough to accommodate the banner. Slip the banner into the slits and glue in place; let dry. Glue tinsel garland around the edge of the photo on the back; let dry. Then glue in place on the front of the card-stock circle.

Cranberry Garland

Shown on *page 153.*

MATERIALS

- Fresh cranberries
- Fine crafts wire

INSTRUCTIONS

Sort through the cranberries to select the firmest fruit. Slide cranberries onto the desired length of crafts wire. Twist the ends of the wire and arrange on table.

Table Runner

Shown on *page 154.*

MATERIALS

- Wrapping paper
- Decorative paper punch

INSTRUCTIONS

Cut wrapping paper to the desired length and width for the table. Using a curved shape, such as a dinner plate for a template, draw scallops along the entire length of each long edge; cut out. Use the decorative paper punch to punch out a decorative border along each scalloped edge.

Tree Stocking

Shown on *page 155.*

MATERIALS

- Purchased stocking
- Fabric-covered buttons
- Spray adhesive
- Glitter
- Tinsel garlands: blue and green
- Matching sewing thread
- Six small blue ornaments
- Crafts glue

INSTRUCTIONS

Remove the metal loops on the backs of the buttons. Place buttons, face up, on a protected surface; then spray the tops and edges with adhesive. Roll the buttons in glitter; let dry. For

the tree trunk and branches, cut lengths of tinsel garland to fit stocking shape and stitch in place. Stitch the ornaments in place on the tinsel branches. Glue glitter-covered buttons onto the cuff. Stitch a loop of garland on the cuff for hanging. Note: If you are unable to find appropriate buttons, purchase fabric similar to your stockings. Use the fabric to cover button blanks, following the manufacturer's instructions.

Ribbon-Embellished Candles

Shown on *page 156.*

MATERIALS

- Pillar candles
- Coordinating ribbons
- Glue gun and hotmelt adhesive

INSTRUCTIONS

Wrap ribbon around the candle. Hot-glue the ribbon at the back of the candle so the seam doesn't show. The hot glue will melt the wax to help with the adhesion.

Candy-Cane Table Runner

Shown on *page 157.*

MATERIALS

- White polar fleece
- Red polar fleece
- 1 yard beaded fringe
- Fabrics glue
- Red beads

INSTRUCTIONS

Cut a rectangle from white polar fleece 14 inches wide and 24 inches longer than your table or sideboard. Enlarge the candy stripe pattern, *right,* using a photocopier; cut out the pattern. Cut candy stripes from red polar fleece to fit the pattern. Use fabrics glue to adhere the

candy stripes to the runner, placing them approximately 6 inches apart; let dry. Cut two 14-inch lengths of beaded trim, and glue them to the back of each end of the runner. Glue red beads on the front side along each end of the table runner.

Note: For a more permanent runner, eliminate the fabrics glue and secure the red fleece in place by top-stitching with your sewing machine. Use a needle and thread to attach the beaded trim to the table runner.

Candy-Cane Candle Cuff

Shown on *page 157.*

MATERIALS

- Pillar candles
- Double-stick carpet tape
- Candy canes

INSTRUCTIONS

Wrap the candle base with tape. Press the candy canes onto the tape, continuing around the diameter of the candle.

Napkin-Holder Box

Shown on *page 157.*

MATERIALS

- Red wrapping paper
- Two wide ribbons
- Glue gun and hotmelt adhesive

INSTRUCTIONS

Cover a box with wrapping paper. Hot-glue wide ribbon around the center of the box. Hot-glue narrower coordinating ribbon over the first ribbon layer.

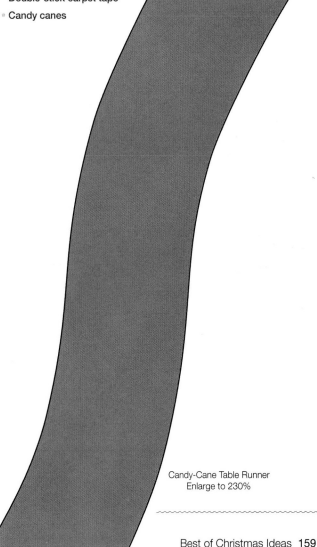

Candy-Cane Table Runner
Enlarge to 230%

quick-as-a-wink

The countdown to Christmas is on. Check out these quick-and-easy ideas for cards, wraps, and decorations, and you'll be ready for the holidays in no time.

SLEIGH BELLS RING, ARE YOU LISTENING?

JINGLE BELLS ARE A TRIED-AND-TRUE HOLIDAY CLASSIC. THIS YEAR, USE THEM IN A FEW UNEXPECTED WAYS TO JAZZ UP YOUR CHRISTMAS DECOR. **NOW CAN YOU HEAR THEM RINGING?**

WRITTEN BY **KRISTIN SCHMITT**   DESIGNED BY **WADE SCHERRER**   PHOTOGRAPHED BY **GREG SCHEIDEMANN**

Card Display Big bells can be used for more than their good looks and sweet sound. Tip them over to create the perfect perch for your holiday cards. This stand is a cinch to construct, and its designer look fits right at home on a mantel or tabletop.

CELEBRATE THE **HOLIDAY SEASON** WITH THE JINGLE JANGLE OF BELLS.

Holiday Card This card, *above*, will jingle all the way to your recipient's mailbox. Simple grosgrain ribbon frames a neat square of layered handmade papers. To complete the look, arrange and glue miniature bells in a wreath shape and top them off with a tidy bow.

Table Runner A standard table runner, *right*, goes glam when a variety of bells are aligned to spell out your favorite holiday word, whether it's Joy, Love, Hope, or Peace. For extra jingle, create a border of bells along both ends of the runner.

Frames Red and silver bells dress up ordinary painted wood frames, *right*. Try outlining the frame with small bells, or create an elegant top for your frame by placing three sizes of bells together.

INSTRUCTIONS BEGIN ON PAGE 168.

1. Centerpiece

MATERIALS
- Large jingle bells
- Green spray paint
- Greenery
- Apples
- Bowl

INSTRUCTIONS
Spray-paint the bells; let dry. Arrange the greenery, bells, and apples in a bowl.

2. Card Display

MATERIALS
- Shallow container
- Narrow and medium-width ribbon
- Glue gun and hotmelt adhesive
- Florist's foam
- Natural or artificial greenery
- Hacksaw
- Seven 3⅜-inch jingle bells
- Drill
- Green spray paint
- ⅛-inch-diameter dowel
- Red bells in assorted sizes
- Florist's wire

INSTRUCTIONS
Hot-glue the medium-width ribbon around the sides of the container; then glue the narrow ribbon over it. Hot-glue florist's foam inside the container and fill with greenery.

Using a hacksaw, cut slits in the top of each large bell. Drill a ⅛-inch diameter hole in the bottom of each bell. Spray-paint the bells green; let dry. Insert a 3-inch length of dowel into the hole at the bottom of each bell and reinforce with hot glue. Insert the bells into the arrangement and slide cards into the bell slits.

Thread assorted-size red bells onto 12-inch lengths of florist's wire to create clusters of berries, leaving a 4- to 6-inch length of bare wire. Twist the wire into a loop and twist again to secure the bells in place. Push the wire ends into the florist's foam.

3. Holiday Card

MATERIALS

- Jingle bells
- Green scrapbooking paper
- Glue gun and hotmelt adhesive
- Narrow ribbon
- White card stock
- Crafts knife
- Silver paper
- Double-stick tape
- Crafts glue

INSTRUCTIONS

Arrange bells in a circle to determine the size of the finished wreath, and draw the circle on the green paper to use as a template. Hot-glue the bells on the green paper covering the drawn circle. Make a bow from ribbon and hot-glue in place.

To create the basic card, cut a piece of card stock the desired size and fold in half. Use a crafts knife to cut a square opening in the front of the card. Cut a mat from a piece of silver paper to fit inside the card front opening. Use tape to adhere the silver mat on the back side of the card front. Tape the green paper with the wreath on the back side of the card front, centering the wreath in the opening. Create a ribbon frame around the card front window and adhere it with glue.

4. Frames

MATERIALS

- Purchased photo frames
- Medium-width ribbon
- Crafts glue
- Glue gun and hotmelt adhesive
- Jingle bells

INSTRUCTIONS

Use crafts glue to apply ribbon around edges of the photo frame; let dry. Hot-glue bells to the frame.

5. Table Runner

MATERIALS

- Green fabric or purchased table runner
- Matching sewing thread
- Jingle bells in two sizes
- Medium-width ribbon

INSTRUCTIONS

If sewing a table runner, determine the length and width desired. Cut fabric, allowing for hemming the edges. Hem all four sides. Determine the placement of the letters to spell out the word "Joy" on one end of the table runner and sew small bells in place. Sew a length of ribbon across the end of the runner. Sew large bells along the center of the ribbon and the edge of the runner.

6. Candleholders

MATERIALS

- Assorted-size candleholders
- Spray primer
- Green spray paint
- Florist's wire
- Jingle bells
- Glue gun and hotmelt adhesive

INSTRUCTIONS

Prime and paint the candle-holders, allowing drying time between coats. Cut a length of florist's wire 2 inches longer than the circumference of the candleholder. String bells on the wire and, if desired, hot-glue the back side of each bell to secure. Leave a 1-inch section of wire at each end. Bend the wire, wrap the bells around the candleholder, and twist the ends of the wire to secure.

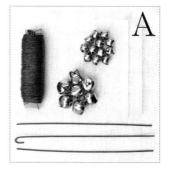

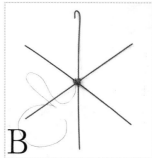

7. Snowflakes

MATERIALS

- 16-gauge crafts wire
- Needle-nose pliers
- Fine crafts wire
- Glue gun and hotmelt adhesive
- Assorted 9-mm- to 1-inch-diameter jingle bells

INSTRUCTIONS

(A) Cut three 6- to 8-inch lengths of 16-gauge crafts wire. Using needle-nose pliers, bend one of the wires to make a hook for hanging. (B) Cross the wire pieces in the center, wrap with fine crafts wire to secure in a spoke shape, and reinforce the wire with hot glue. (C) Hot-glue one bell over the center intersection of the wire assembly. Slide bells on each wire spoke, securing them on the back side with hot glue. Trim the remaining wires.

graceful
garlands

Grab some sparkling tinsel or strings of beads and make a spirited decorative statement with festive holiday garlands.

WRITTEN BY **KRISTIN SCHMITT**   PRODUCED BY **KAREN LIDBECK-BRENT**   PHOTOGRAPHED BY **MICHAEL PARTENIO**

Trim the Tree

Use a plethora of garlands to create the appearance of a tree dressed in ornaments without having to hang them one by one. To make the sparkling star atop this decked-out tree, glue wooden kabob spears into the shape of a star and cover the sticks with tinsel garland.

Tabletop Treasure

Create a tabletop decoration with a few strands of beaded garland and a handful of branches. Tuck florist's foam into an urn or flowerpot and arrange bare branches in the foam (first coat them with white spray paint or snow spray if desired). To complete the decoration, cover the foam with moss, tie a holiday bow around the top of the container, and drape the branches with garlands.

Dining in Style

Mark a special spot for each diner at your holiday table with festive chair dressings. Hang a noteworthy ornament (such as this sparkling paper bell) from a strip of tinsel garland, tie the ends of the garland to the top of the chair, and embellish with evergreen sprigs.

Wrapped in Light

Cast a warm holiday glow atop the mantelpiece with this glittering wreath. Using a large straw crafts wreath for the base, wrap a piece of wire around the top to create a hanger. Then wind a 50-count strand of white lights tightly around the wreath, positioning the lights so they point in all directions and securing them with floral U-shape pins. Next, cover the wreath by wrapping it with tinsel garland and securing the ends with U-shape pins, taking care to avoid the electrical cord. Pine branches and a Christmas bow wired at the top add a festive finish.

Window Dressings

Add a pretty holiday swag to your window treatments using large beaded garland. Drape a couple of garland strings over the curtain rod, securing them with tape on the back side of the rod. For a finishing touch—like the tassel on a drapery cord—wire elegant glass balls to the garland ends and top the balls with greenery.

Stairway Showcase

For a twist on the traditional banister, try this garland accent. Wire double swags of green tinsel garland at intervals up the banister rail and tie on ornaments dangling from silver ribbon. To add clusters of greenery and holly, tightly wrap wire around the railing for each cluster and tuck cuttings securely beneath the wire.

Blue Ice

Sparkling white snow, a brilliant blue sky lit by the pale winter sun, silver ice coating bare trees and hanging as icicles from eaves—these are the colors outside at Christmas.

Bring these icy hues indoors to create a holiday scene that's perfectly in tune with nature and as refreshing as a walk in the snow. To create the look, gather up the most glimmering bits and pieces of paper, fabric, and ornaments and get started on a Christmas that will make you feel anything but blue.

Written by VERONICA LORSON FOWLER Designed by WANDA VENTLING
Photographed by GREG SCHEIDEMANN

WARMEST WISHES FOR A COOL YULE

You'd never guess it, but these truly cool snowflake ornaments, *opposite* and *on middle package*, were made by cutting snowflake shapes from two layers of blue card stock glued together and topped with a mixture of white glue and glitter embossing powder. The smaller, more delicate snowflake on the top package was made by quilling, which is an old-fashioned process of curling and folding narrow strips of paper.

HAVE A BALL

Or dozens of them! This wreath appears intricate but is actually quite simple to make. Just wrap a foam wreath with white or pale blue ribbon. Then hot-glue

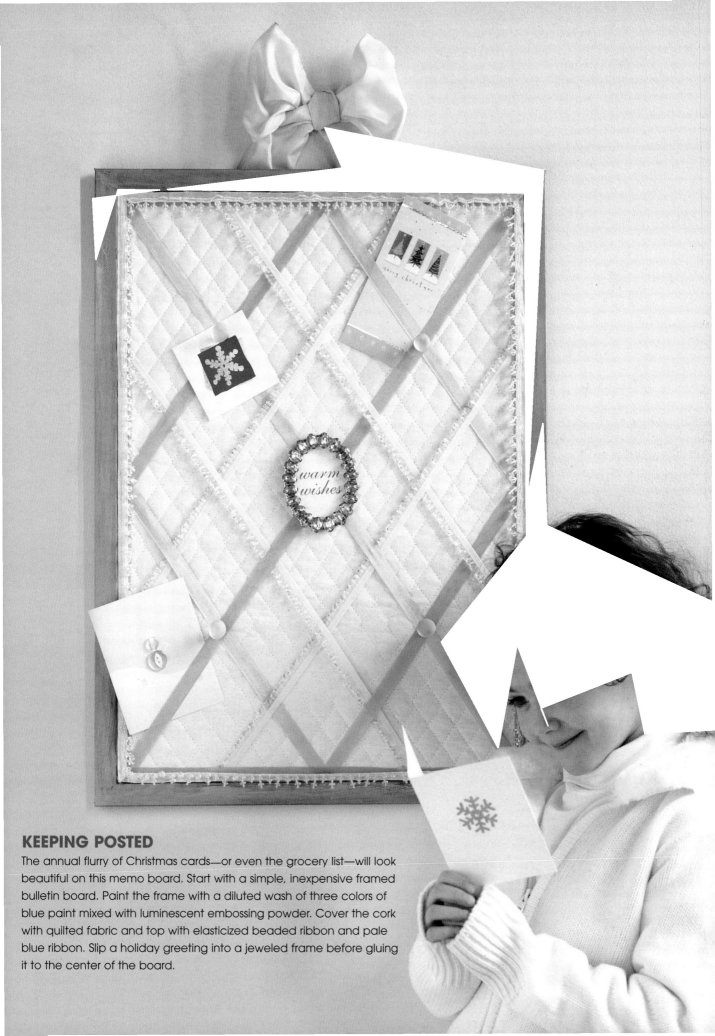

KEEPING POSTED

The annual flurry of Christmas cards—or even the grocery list—will look beautiful on this memo board. Start with a simple, inexpensive framed bulletin board. Paint the frame with a diluted wash of three colors of blue paint mixed with luminescent embossing powder. Cover the cork with quilted fabric and top with elasticized beaded ribbon and pale blue ribbon. Slip a holiday greeting into a jeweled frame before gluing it to the center of the board.

DINING WITH JEWELS

Nothing sets the mood for the holidays like a pretty table. Our runner is a snap to make with a fat band of blue sateen edging wispy white fabric. Beading from a crafts store adds a dressy holiday finish.

BANNER HOLIDAY

This ornament makes a perfect package topper or a keepsake gift at a Christmas party. Just print your chosen greeting onto card stock and cut it into a strip using scallop-edge decorative scissors. Wrap the strip around the ornament, gluing the overlapped edges together. Add stick-on gems to the strip for a bit of sparkle.

A TRUE BLUE STOCKING

What could be prettier than a Christmas stocking turned out in lovely pale blue velveteen? This stocking takes on a mod flair with a cuff of oh-so-soft white fake fur and a tiny sparkling star made from white icy beads.

feeling blue for the holidays

Here are some other ways to go blue this year.
❋ Stick to the same intensity and tone of blue for consistency. We used a pale blue-gray, but you could try a rich midnight blue or a brilliant royal blue.
❋ Take the blue even further than fabrics and a wreath. Wrap all your gifts in blue, white, and silver. Spruce up the bathroom with white towels custom-trimmed in silver and blue. Frost all your greenery, even your tree.
❋ Bring out old silver to go with the blue. Fill silver bowls with blue or white glass balls. A silver tray would look gorgeous displaying blue glassware—just for show—or mounded with pinecones coated with silver paint.
❋ Add instant gleam with a can of chrome-look spray paint. Give gone-shabby ornaments a quick coat to coordinate with the tree. Turn a basket into a silvery receptacle for gifts.

INSTRUCTIONS BEGIN ON PAGE 182.

QUILLED SNOWFLAKE

Shown on *page 177*.

MATERIALS
White typing paper
Crafts glue
Tweezers
Sheer white ribbon

INSTRUCTIONS
Cut twenty-five $\frac{1}{4}\times8\frac{1}{2}$-inch strips from white typing paper. Fold one strip in half to measure $4\frac{1}{4}$ inches. Open the strip up and bring each end in to the center fold to make a strip that measures $\frac{1}{4}\times2\frac{1}{8}$ inches. Glue the layers of the strip together for $1\frac{1}{4}$ inches, beginning at the center fold. Curl the unglued ends of the paper strip in opposite directions, creating a scroll shape. Repeat with five additional strips to make six pieces.

Stack two strips of paper together, hold the center with tweezers, and overlap the ends slightly. Put a dot of glue on one side of the end, and pinch to form an oval; let glue set. Make six ovals.

Using the same method, make six smaller ovals for the snowflake tips, using one strip for each oval.

For the center, roll a strip into a tight circle, holding the center with tweezers. Use a dot of glue to secure the end; let glue set. Arrange the snowflake pieces and large ovals around the center circle, alternating the shapes. Glue the shapes to the center circle and to each other; let glue set. Glue a small oval between the scrolls at the end of the arm.

Let ornament dry overnight. Thread ribbon to create the hanging loop.

HAVE A BALL WREATH

Shown on *page 178*.

MATERIALS
Plastic-foam wreath
2-inch-wide white ribbon
Glue gun and hotmelt adhesive
Ball ornaments in a variety of colors
    and sizes

INSTRUCTIONS
Wrap ribbon around wreath, slightly overlapping the edges to completely cover; hot-glue to secure. Hot-glue the large ball ornaments to the wreath, positioning the balls at various locations and distributing colors evenly. Continue adding smaller ornaments, hot-gluing the balls to the wreath or to each other. Use the smallest ornaments to fill open areas.

KEEPING POSTED

Shown on *page 179*.

MATERIALS
Bulletin board with wooden frame
Blue acrylic paint
Luminescent embossing powder
Paintbrush
White quilted fabric
Spray adhesive
$\frac{1}{2}$-inch-wide blue and white ribbons
Stapler
Glue gun and hotmelt adhesive
Computer, printer, and white card
    stock
Small crystal frame
4 decorative pushpins
$1\frac{1}{4}$ yards of 5-inch-wide wire-edge
    ribbon

INSTRUCTIONS
Paint the bulletin-board frame using blue paint and embossing powder. Let dry.

Cut a piece of quilted fabric to cover the cork area. Spray the back of the fabric with adhesive, place it adhesive side down on the cork, and press into place.

Cut ribbon to stretch diagonally across the board. Weave ribbons over and under; staple ends to the frame. Cut ribbon and beaded trim to edge cork. Lay ribbon over the fabric edges and woven ribbon ends; hot-glue in place.

Use a computer to print a message in coordinating ink on white card stock, sizing the text to fit the crystal frame. Cut out the message and insert in frame. Hot-glue the frame on the center of the board.

To finish, tie a bow of wire-edge ribbon to the center top. Place pushpins at ribbon intersections to hold cards.

CENTERPIECE

Shown on *page 180*.

MATERIALS
Evergreen sprigs
Artificial snow spray
Clear glass container
Clear glass gems
Acrylic ice chips or cubes
White flowers
White ribbon

INSTRUCTIONS
Spray evergreen sprigs with artificial snow; let dry. Fill the glass container with glass gems and acrylic ice; then add white flowers and evergreen sprigs. Tie ribbon around the container.

DINING WITH JEWELS

Shown on *page 180*.

MATERIALS
White sheer fabric
White lining fabric
Blue shiny fabric
1 yard of beaded trim

INSTRUCTIONS
Determine the desired finished length of the table runner; subtract 6 inches. Cut an 11-inch-wide rectangle for the center of the runner from the white sheer fabric and the white lining fabric. Allow for $\frac{1}{2}$-inch seam allowances. With wrong sides together, stitch the rectangles along the outside edges.

From blue fabric, cut two $4\frac{1}{2}$-inch-wide side border strips 10 inches longer than the center section and two $4\frac{1}{2}\times21$-inch end border strips for the ends.

With right sides together, sew the side borders to the center, starting and stopping $\frac{1}{2}$ inch from the short edges of the center section; (each border will extend beyond the ends to allow for mitered corners). Press seam allowances away from the center section. Sew an end border strip to each short edge in the same manner. Press seam allowances toward

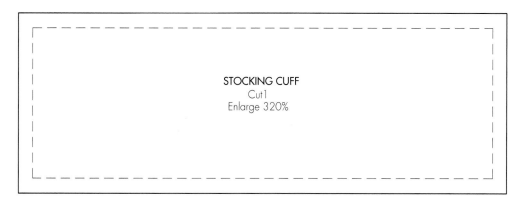

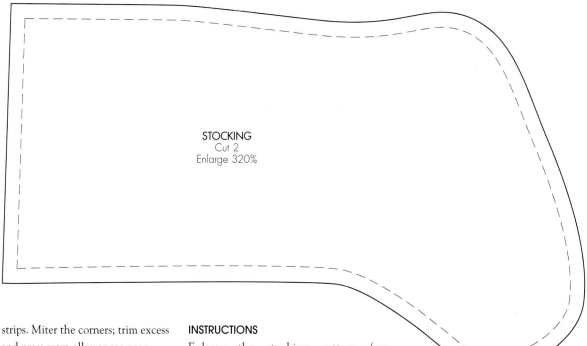

border strips. Miter the corners; trim excess fabric, and press seam allowances open.

Use the pieced front as a pattern for the matching bottom. Pin and sew beaded trim to the runner's ends. With right sides together, sew the front to the back, leaving a 3-inch opening on one end. Trim seams and corners. Turn the table runner right side out; press. Slip-stitch opening closed.

A TRUE BLUE STOCKING

Shown on *page 181*.

MATERIALS

⅝ yard of blue velveteen fabric
⅝ yard of blue lining fabric
Two 18-inch lengths of 3-inch-wide faux fur trim
Matching sewing thread
2½-inch-diameter beaded snowflake

INSTRUCTIONS

Enlarge the stocking pattern (see Stocking and Stocking Cuff *above*) using a photocopier. Cut out the patterns. When sewing pieces together, use a ½-inch seam allowance with right sides facing.

Cut a stocking front and back and a cuff from blue velveteen and a matching lining stocking front and back and cuff.

Sew the stocking front to the back, leaving the top edge open. Trim the seams; clip the curves. Turn the stocking right side out. Repeat with stocking lining pieces, but do not turn right side out. Slip the lining inside the stocking with wrong sides facing, aligning the top edges. Baste the top edges together.

Cut a 1½×6-inch strip of blue velveteen for the hanging loop; press under ¼ inch on each long edge. Fold the strip in half lengthwise, aligning the pressed edges; press again and stitch shut. Fold the strip in half to form a loop and stitch to the top edge.

Sew the cuff to the cuff lining at the long

bottom edge; press seam allowances open. Sew the trim to the cuff.

Cut a 3×18-inch strip of blue velveteen for trim binding. Fold the binding strip in half with wrong sides together; press. Position the binding strip along the top edge of the cuff; sew using a ½-inch seam allowance. Fold the binding over the top edge; edge-stitch in place.

Fold the lining to the back side of the cuff; baste the top edges together. Stitch the short ends of the cuff together to create a circle; press seams open.

Slip the cuff inside the stocking with the right side of the cuff facing the stocking lining. Align the top edges; sew the cuff to the stocking. Fold the cuff over the right side of the stocking. Hand-sew a snowflake to the stocking front.

wrapping up
the season

Create holiday paper crafts as unique as the people receiving them. These festive gift wraps, tags, and cards are easily assembled with embellishments found in the scrapbooking aisles at your local crafts store.

❄ sing along

Lucky recipients will burst into song when they receive a trio of stacked gift boxes adorned with rhinestone-studded tags. Polka-dot paper and green ribbon add flair to the packages, while round white tags encircled with green card stock and ruby rhinestones show off the words to a favorite holiday tune.

WRITTEN BY **CAROL LINNAN**   PHOTOGRAPHED BY **GREG SCHEIDEMANN**

Spice up plain gift boxes and bags with scrapbooking paper that's perfect for wrapping holiday gifts. Add the finishing touches with ribbons, jewels, buttons, and bows.

❄ dressed to impress

Decorate a red gift box with shimmering rhinestones and strands of white faux pearls tied with a satin bow. A red gift bag looks striking adorned in delicate paper snowflakes and pearls.

itty-bitty box

Small in size but big on charm, this itty-bitty box is personalized on the front with a metal nameplate, so there'll be no mistaking who is Santa's favorite.

trimming the tree

Convey your holiday sentiments with a Christmas-tree card decorated with tiny ornaments, *above*. Fold a piece of crimson card stock in half; then add a handmade tree and a tied ribbon to the cover. Cute ornaments complete the joyful holiday greeting.

a berry happy holiday

The beauty of this gift tag, *right*, lies in the details. Affix a rectangle of checkered scrapbooking paper to a precut tag and add self-adhesive holly and berries. Use a bold marker to pen the recipient's name on the tag.

ornamental charm

Traditional Christmas wishes benefit from a retro twist with bright, festive colors. Create a frame by attaching prestitched ribbon to folded card stock. For a finishing touch, a charm suspended from string takes the place of the "o" in Noel.

sensational stripes

Papers with candy-cane stripes and red polka dots on white fit the season, *above*. Finish a package with a purchased holly-trimmed frame setting off a festive "ho, ho, ho" greeting.

buttons and bows

Dress a plain white box in perfect party attire by gluing on playful red buttons, *right*. Border the buttons with holiday-hue striped ribbons and finish with a lime-green pinstripe bow.

Sing Along

MATERIALS

- 3 gift boxes
- Rub-on letters
- 2-inch white round tags
- Glue gun and hotmelt adhesive
- 5- and 7-mm ruby rhinestones
- Green card stock
- Medium-width ribbon

INSTRUCTIONS

Rub the lettering onto the center of each white tag. Glue the ruby rhinestones around the edges of each tag, alternating the sizes. Cut a green card-stock circle ¼ inch larger than the white tags; glue the circle to the back of each tag. Thread ribbon through the hole.

Dressed to Impress

GIFT BOX MATERIALS

- Red mailer box
- 13-mm round rhinestones
- Glue gun and hotmelt adhesive
- Pearl beaded trim
- Wide satin ribbon

INSTRUCTIONS

Place several rhinestones on top of the box and hot-glue them in place. Wrap strands of pearl beading around box vertically, and glue them at back of box. Using satin ribbon, tie a simple knot around center of beading; trim the ends.

GIFT BAG MATERIALS

- Red gift bag
- Quilled paper snowflakes
- White crafts glue
- 7-mm round faux half pearls
- Paper punch
- Striped satin ribbon
- White satin ribbon

INSTRUCTIONS

Peel off the adhesive backing on the snowflakes and press them to the front of the bag. Apply a small amount of glue to each pearl, and glue it to the bag around the snowflakes. Using a paper punch, make holes at the top of the bag. Layer the striped ribbon with the white ribbon, thread through the punched holes, and tie into a bow.

Trimming the Tree

MATERIALS

- Red card stock
- Green card stock
- Glue stick or double-stick tape
- Self-adhesive mini pop-dots
- Ornament stickers
- Narrow satin ribbon
- Rub-on phrase

INSTRUCTIONS

Cut red card stock 7½×7½ inches and fold in half. Referring to the photo for the shape, cut out a tree from the green card stock. Adhere the tree to the front of the card. Press dots to the back of each ornament. Press in place on the tree. Wrap ribbon around the front flap of the card. Tie in a bow. Use a rub-on phrase to add a greeting.

Itty-Bitty Box

MATERIALS

- Small gift box
- Green scrapbooking paper
- White crafts glue
- Narrow ribbon
- White card stock
- Metal label embellishment

INSTRUCTIONS

Wrap the box and lid with green paper. Glue ribbon to the lid edges. Cut a white paper shape to fit within the label. Write the recipient's name, and glue the tag to the center of the label. Adhere the label to the package with glue.

INSTRUCTIONS

Cut scrapbooking paper to 6×10 inches, fold in half width-wise. Cut card stock to measure 3½×5 inches. Cut ribbon into four equal lengths. Cut each end at an angle to create a 3½×5-inch frame. Type the letters n, e, and l on a computer, allowing enough space for the charm to represent the o in noel. Glue the ribbon to the card-stock rectangle to make a frame. Press the frame in place in the center of the folded striped card using tape. Tie embroidery floss to the charm and finish with a bow. Glue the ornament in place on the front of the card to complete the word.

Buttons and Bows

MATERIALS

- White mailer box
- Glue gun and hotmelt adhesive
- ¾-inch red buttons
- Medium-width ribbons

INSTRUCTIONS

Evenly space and hot-glue the red buttons on the center of the box. Cut two lengths of ribbon, wrap a length around the box on either side of the buttons, and hot-glue in place. Tie a simple bow around the box.

A Berry Happy Holiday

MATERIALS

- Checked scrapbooking paper
- Glue stick or double-stick tape
- 2×4-inch precut rectangle shipping tag
- Quilled holly and berries trim

INSTRUCTIONS

Cut a 1½×3-inch piece of scrapbooking paper. Use a glue stick or double-stick tape to adhere the paper to the center of the tag. Peel the self-adhesive backing from the holly embellishment and press onto the corner of the tag.

Sensational Stripes

MATERIALS

- Tall square box with lid
- Striped and polka-dot scrapbooking paper
- Wide green ribbon
- Glue gun and hotmelt adhesive
- Mini frame
- Holly-berry trim

INSTRUCTIONS

Wrap base of box in striped paper and lid of box in polka-dot paper. Wrap ribbon around box vertically; hot-glue in place. Wrap a piece of ribbon around a loop of ribbon to make a bow, and glue it to the lid. Hot-glue holly-berry trim to the corner of the frame; then glue the frame to the gift.

Ornamental Charm

MATERIALS

- Striped scrapbooking paper
- Off-white card stock
- Prestitched grosgrain ribbon
- Crafts glue
- Double-stick tape
- Embroidery floss
- Ornament charm

sources

Many of the materials and items used in this book can be found at fabrics, hobby, and crafts stores. To find a specific retailer near you, contact the manufacturers listed below.

Page 6
Easy Elegance
Wallpaper wrapping: Wallquest, #TW70101; www.wallquest .com, Thibaut, #T-9396, 800/223- 0704; www.thibautdesign .com, Waverly, #5502764; www.waverly.com. Narrow checked and striped ornament ribbons: Making Memories, 800/286-5263; www.makingmemories.com. All package ribbons: Midori, 800/659-3049; www.midoriribbon.com. Label: Artisan Labels, #23353 by Making Memories, 800/286-5263; www .makingmemories.com. Paper place-mat doily: Royal Lace, 800/436-4919; www.theroyalstore.com. Dress: DressKids, 888/373-7754; www.dresskids.com. Damask pillow fabric: Waverly, #649973; www.waverly.com. Tree-skirt trim: Calico Corners, 800/213-6366; www.calicocorners.com. Star ornaments and tree topper: 3-D star kits by Paper Source, 312/906-9678; www.paper-source.com. (We added red paper cutouts to our tree topper.) Die-cut shape for felt surround on round package: AccuCut, 800/288-1670; www.accucut.com. Felt: National Nonwovens, 800/333-3469; www.woolfelt.com. Christmas balls: Better Homes and Gardens® collection from Roman, 800/729-7662; www.roman.com. Decoupage medium, acrylic paint, and paint-tip set: Plaid Enterprises, 800/842-4197; www.plaidenterprises.com. Napkins: Plum Party, 718/433-2482; www.plumparty.com. Rhinestone flower brad: Scrappy Creations. Scalloped lace border: Mrs. Grossman's Paper Company, 800/429-4549; www.mrsgrossmans.com. Eye bead: Darice, 866/432-7423; www.darice.com. Tree die cut: Sizzix by Provo Craft, 877/355-4766; www.sizzix.com.

Page 16
Merry & Bright
Ribbons and wrapping papers: Midori, 800/659-3049; www .midoriribbon.com. All flowers: provided by California Cut Flower Commission; www.ccfc.org. Pillow: TJMaxx, 800/285-6299; www. tjmaxx.com. Chair: Design Centre Collections, 515/334-0123. Candlesticks, throw on chair, table votives, stemware, hurricanes, and red pillar candle: Target Stores, 800/800-8800; www.target. com. Pillow: Marshalls, 888/627-74257; www .marshallsonline.com. Chair: Ethan Allen; www.ethanallen.com. Christmas balls: Better Homes and Gardens® collection from Roman, 800/729-7662; www.roman.com. Creamware containers: Hager from Michaels, 800/642-3049; www.michaels.com. Napkins: World Market, 877/967-5362; www.worldmarket.com. Chargers: Midwest of Cannon Falls; www.midwestofcannonfalls .com. Buffet mirror: Better Homes and Gardens® Collection from Home Interiors, www.homeinteriors.com. Green stripe candles: Seasonal Concepts, 800/899-2686; www.seasonalconcepts.com.

Page 28
Swedish Noel
Table runner: Williams-Sonoma, 877/812-6235; www .williams-sonoma.com. Ribbon on runner: Bucilla red silk, available at crafts stores. Snowflake punch: EK Success; www.eksuccess .com. Wrapping paper: IKEA, 800/434-4532; www.ikea.com.

Plates and bowls: Crate and Barrel, 800/996-9960; www .crateandbarrel.com.
Dog on mantel: Target Stores, 800/800-8800; www.target.com.

Page 40
Tradition with a Twist
Ribbon—Midori, Inc.; 800/659-3049; www.midoriribbon .com. Fabric—Kravet; 888/457-2838; www.kravet.com [T]. Trims—Kravet; 888/457-2838; www.kravet.com [T] and Wal-Mart; 800/881-9180; www.walmart.com (product lines vary). Ornaments—Roman, Inc.; 630/705-4600; www.roman.com. Cones, glitter ornaments, toile tins—Wal-Mart; 800/925-6278; www.walmart.com (product lines vary). Lime plates, hurricanes, candles, green pillow, silverware, stemware, napkins—Pier 1 Imports; 800/245-4595; www.pier1.com. Silver tray—Hobby Lobby; 800/323-9204; www.hobbylobby.com.

Page 52
A Warm & Cozy Christmas
Feather trees—Seasons of Cannon Falls; 800/776-2075; www.seasonsofcannonfalls.com. Burlap for tree skirt, fabric for stockings—Hancock Fabrics, 877/322-7427; www.hancockfabrics .com. Felt, ribbon, trims—Hobby Lobby; 800/323-9204; www .hobbylobby.com. Felt balls—Tinsel Trading Co.; 212/730-1030; www.tinseltrading.com. Scrabble paper, photo envelopes— EK Success; 800/524-1349; www.eksuccess.com for retailers. Letter stickers—Making Memories; 801/294-0430; www .makingmemories.com. Paper for cone ornaments—K & Co.; www.kandcompany.com.

Page 64
Tradition with a Twist of Lime
Porch urns: The Weed Lady, Fenton, MI, 810/655-2723. Black chair and settee: Oly Studio, 510/644-1870; www.olystudio.com. Pillow, bottles on mantel, and votive candles: Pottery Barn, 800/922-5507; www.potterybarn.com. Mirror and stockings: Ballard Designs, 800/367-2775. Rug: Woven Treasures, 248/723-8888; www.woventreasures.net. Mantel urns: Europe Direct Warehouse, 248/691-9155; www.europedirectwarehouse.com. Chairs: Crate and Barrel, 800/996-9960; www.crateandbarrel.com. Checkered containers on table: Mackenzie-Childs, 888/665-1999; www.mackenzie-childs.com. All remaining items: available through S.L. Smith Design, 248/420-9039.

Page 72
Fresh, Fast & Fabulous
Florists Review Christmas Traditions: Florists Review, 800/367-4708; www.floristsreview.com/betterhomes.

Page 88
Holiday Harvest
Feather tree: The Feather Tree Company, 608/837-7669; www.feathertrees.com. Orange plates: Pier 1, 800/245-4595; www.pier1.com. Glass balls: The Elizabeth Burdick Collection, Woodbury, CT, 203/263-0036. Hartland glass hurricane: Simon Pearce, 877/452-7763; www.simonpearce.com. Pinecone candle: Crafted Candles, 800/635-0274; www.craftedcandles.com. Nested baskets: (12-inch square handled, 11-inch bowl, and 9-inch bowl), Longaberger Basket Company, 740/322-7800; www.longaberger.com. Ceramic basket: B. Bourgeois Antiques, 203/263-7101. Pinecones: Moosehorn River Products, 218/389-6300; www.moosehornriver.com and Rocky Mountain Pine Cones, 877/539-7949; www.rockymountainpinecones.com.

Page 96
Outdoor Decor
Moravian stars: Old Salem Museums and Gardens, 888/653-7253; www.oldsalem.com. Shimmering spheres, brown corded lights: Bronner's Christmas Wonderland, 989/652-9935; www.bronners.com. Grapevine spheres, grapevine trees: Grape Vine Products, 800/772-0674; www.grapevineproducts.com.

Page 108
Simple Sweets
Glass candy dishes and Initially Yours sparkle letters—Seasons of Cannon Falls, 800/776-2075; www.seasonsofcannonfalls.com. Cake stand—Cost Plus World Market, 800/267-8758; www.costplus.com. Crystal beads on napkin tips—Crafts, Etc!; 800/888-0321; www.craftsetc.com.

Page 116
Gourmet Gifts
Ramekins, cheese spreader, dish towel, green tray—Crate & Barrel, 800/996-9960; www.crateandbarrel.com (product lines vary). Sticky felt, white tags, streamer paper, jingle bells—Michaels Stores, Inc., 800/642-4235; www.michaels.com. Cording, labels—Paper Source, 888/727-3711; www.paper-source.com. Ribbon on jelly jar, felt, velvet, fake fur—Jo-Ann Stores, Inc., 877/465-6266; www.jo-ann.com. Sticker paper for jelly jar, tag and leaves for vinegar bottle, tags for Santa bags, paper and dots for wreath tin, paper for cookie tray—Outstamping Designs, 215 5th St., West Des Moines, IA 50265; 515/277-5519; www.outstampingdesigns.com. Vinegar bottle, muffin basket—Pier 1 Imports, 800/245-4595; www.pier1.com. Ribbon on vinegar bottle, Santa bags, and wreath tin, candy box paper—Midori, Inc., 800/659-3049; www.midoriribbon.com. Ribbon on candy box—Tinsel Trading Co., 212/730-1030; www.tinseltrading.com.

Page 132
Serving Up Style
Rectangular table, Swedish Home collection—Ethan Allen; www.ethanallen.com. White chairs, gold chargers, green candles, red napkins—Pier 1 Imports, 800/245-4595; www.pier1.com. Red Dot and 'Tis the Season dishes—Rosanna, Inc., 866/767-2662; www.rosannainc.com. Glass candlesticks—Target Stores, 800/800-8800; www.target.com (product lines vary). Ornaments—Roman, Inc., 630/529-3000; www.roman.com. Chandelle Frosted flatware and Colore goblet—Lenox, 800/223-4311; www.lenox.com. Simple Additions white square dishes—The Pampered Chef. For more information or to contact a local Kitchen Consultant in your area, call 800/266-5562 or visit www.pamperedchef.com. Green glasses and napkins, red votive holders—Cost Plus World Market, 800/267-8758; www.costplus.com. Chantel ribbon on green place mats—Offray; www.offray.com for retailers. Melamine plates and cups, kids' table flatware, clear dishes—Kmart, 800/866-0086; www.kmart.com (product lines vary). Chipboard boxes, floral foam cones—Hobby Lobby, 800/323-9204; www.hobbylobby.com. White berries and green ribbon—Papourri, 1751 28th St., West Des Moines, IA, 50266; 515/223-7265. Lollipops—Hammond's Candies, 888/226-3999; www.hammondscandies.com. Burgundy Quilted Beaded Shorty slipcovers—Sure Fit; 800/506-6750; www.surefit.com. Rondure flatware—Dansk; 800/293-2675; www.dansk.com. Douppioni Silk fabric for tablecloth—Jo-Ann Stores, Inc., 877/465-6266; www.jo-ann.com. Chinese screen—Fusion Furniture, 515/244-2303; www.fusionfurnituregallery.com.

Page 142
Blue Christmas
Silk—A.S. International; www.indiamart.com/asinter. Wire pom-pom trim—Black Ink, 101 Charles St., Boston, MA 02114; 617/723-3883. Sheer ribbon—Mokuba NY; 55 W. 39th St., New York, NY 10018; 212/869-8900. Iron-on crystal letters, bead tassels—Michaels Crafts, 800/642-423; www.michaels.com. Rub-on decals, 24-gauge blue-coated copper wire—A.C. Moore, www.acmoore.com. Beads—Beadworks International, Inc., 800/232-3761; www.beadworks.com. Silver beads—Blue Moon Beads, 800/377-6715; www.bluemoonbeads.com. Letter charm—Making Memories, 801/294-0430; www.makingmemories.com.

Page 150
3 Seasonal Settings
Tables and chairs: Abante Contemporary Furnishings, 515/278-8621 and World Market, 877/967-5362; www.worldmarket.com. Hand-dyed felt: Weeks Dye Works, 919/772-9166; www.weeksdyeworks.com. Candy canes: Candy Corner USA, 800/721-7714; www.candycornerusa.com. Peppermint sprinkles: Stonewall Kitchen, 800/207-5267; www.stonewallkitchen.com. Feather trees: Bethany Lowe Designs, Inc., 309/944-6214; www.bethanylowe.com.

page 162
Jingle Bells
Jingle bells: Terry's Village, 800/876-5822; www.terrysvillage.com., Oriental Trading Company 800/875-8480; www.orientaltrading.com and Art Cove, Ltd., 718/381-7782; www.artcove.com.

Page 176

Blue Ice

Fabric and ribbons—Jo-Ann Fabrics; www.jo-ann.com.
Ornament wreath—Seasons of Cannon Falls, 800/776-2075;
www.seasonsofcannonfalls.com. Beads, embossing powder,
and crafts supplies—Michaels Stores, Inc., 800/642-4235;
www.michaels.com.

Page 184

Wrapping Up the Season

Rub-on letters: Scrapworks, 801/363-1010; www.scrapworks
.com. Ruby rhinestones: The Beadery, 401/539-2432; www
.thebeadery.com. Rub-on letters: Making Memories, 801/294-
0430; www.makingmemories.com. Glitter ornaments: EK
Success; www.eksuccess.com. Polka-dot ribbon: Making
Memories, 801/294-0430; www.makingmemories.com.
Quilled holly and snowflakes: Provo Craft, 800/937-7686;
www.provocraft.com. Crystal rhinestones: The Beadery,
401/539-2432; www.thebeadery.com. Oval-shape pearl-
beaded trim: Hobby Lobby, 800/323-9204; www.hobbylobby
.com. Red-and-white striped and polka-dot paper: Melissa
Frances, 905/686-9031; melissafrances.com. Mini frame:
Slide Sentiments by Magic Scraps, 972/238-1838; www
.magicscraps.com. Holly berry trim: EK Success; www
.eksuccess.com. Striped grosgrain ribbon: Doodlebug Design;
www.doodlebug.com.